Lela Rose
PRÊT-A-PARTY

RIZZOLI
NEW YORK

New York · Paris · London · Milan

To Brandon, Grey, and Rosey

CONTENTS

INTRODUCTION

The best party I ever threw almost never happened. A friend's husband asked if I would plan a surprise party for his wife, and at first, I tried to decline. Most of my parties aren't held for specific events; I prefer occasion-less entertaining, where the motivation behind the gathering is just to have fun. Plus, my entertaining style has an offbeat flavor, and I often like to include some eyebrow-raising elements at my parties, so I wasn't sure if this would go over well with an invitation list I could not control.

My friend's husband persisted, however, and then I was hit with an irresistible idea: ever since I moved to New York, I had dreamed of hosting a group for cocktails in the subway. The subway is an emblem of the city with a unique, amazing energy, and taking over unexpected spaces has always appealed to me. This was my chance to give my friend a totally original, unforgettable birthday and have a great time doing it. So I agreed, on the condition that her husband let me plan the entire evening—with no veto power.

I invited guests to meet on a subway platform near our TriBeCa apartment. When people stepped off the train in cocktail attire, their skeptical looks turned to delight as I greeted them with margaritas served in Ball jars wrapped in brown paper bags. We hung out and chatted on the platform while a steel-drum player I had recruited from another subway station serenaded us. As trains pulled in and out, our party drew curious looks and amused smiles from fellow New Yorkers. At the appointed hour, my friend got off the train (her husband having led her downtown on the pretense of a dinner reservation), noticed the unusual revelry, and then broke out into a burst of laughter when she realized that the dressed-up people having a great time on the platform were there for her. We then marched through the city streets back to my apartment, where more cocktails and a seated dinner awaited. But the surprises weren't quite done. After the meal, an amazing drag performer that I had hired for the evening named Candis Cayne emerged through a curtain from the back of the apartment in a vintage Bob Mackie sequined dress. As the cake came out, she sang a racy, Marilyn Monroe-inspired "Happy Birthday" to the birthday girl while guests watched, mouths agape, as she accompanied her singing with whirling cancan kicks. My girlfriend was giddy and beaming the entire time, and despite my original reluctance, it ended up being exactly the kind of party I love: one with an unexpected mix of venues, delicious food, utterly quirky entertainment, and a spirit of pure fun.

Fun rules my life. The joy of creating drives my work as a fashion designer. I want to make clothing that surprises and delights, that is as whimsical as it is beautiful. As a mother, I try to instill in my kids the pleasure of making, imagining, and creating. And I throw parties constantly because, well, they're fun—fun that I can give my guests, but even more importantly, fun for me to plan and put on.

My passion for entertaining started with my mother. She is a fabulous cook who considered opening a restaurant, held dinner parties regularly when I was growing up, and tried out ambitious recipes whenever inspiration struck—making sure that our Grand Marnier soufflés were perfectly risen was more important than us getting to school on time. And my mother never, ever took the ready-made option. She got so much pleasure imagining how to reinvent and repurpose things around our house that store-bought was synonymous with boring. From a very young age, I experienced the delight of figuring out how to create the things I wanted, and I've learned that the magic of transforming ordinary days into occasions of endless possibilities is as exciting for adults as it is for children.

Every fashion collection I design begins with a speck of an idea that can come from anywhere: it can be a color combination, an unusual pattern, or a great meal I've eaten. I then expand and shape that initial idea by pulling in textures, colors, silhouettes, and details until it's a fully realized collection. I plan parties in the same way; every gathering I throw, whether it be for a special evening, a casual get-together over a meal, or an event I've conjured up from scratch, comes from an initial spark that becomes the party theme. This theme dictates what I wear, how I dress the table, the menu, the invitation, and activities. My parties are irreverent mixes of high and low, and they put pleasure above custom. If you want to be inspired and encouraged to throw your own unique parties, whatever they may be, welcome to my world of daring, slightly mischievous nuttiness, where inspiration drives the plans and every day can (and should) be its own occasion.

One thing I sometimes hear people say is "Throwing a party is a lot of work." But I have an utterly different outlook. After years of madcap entertaining—following my whims from industrial rooftops to street parades led by a marching band to subway tunnels, and cajoling my friends and family into taking part in the countless crazy schemes that I've concocted—I've figured out how to make throwing unique gatherings easy and endlessly fun. For me, putting on a party is a time to play. I hope this book leaves you feeling the same way.

My childhood was filled with fun and creativity and this has fueled my drive to design and entertain ever since. Counter-clockwise from top left: My mother and I on the Fourth of July; my homemade "American as Apple Pie" Fourth of July getup; our Christmas "string gift" (see page 57); Easter with live bunnies; my father in tux and slippers at one of my parents' fabulous dinner parties; tracking down the Christmas "string gift" (see page 57); my mother, left, "guzzling with gusto"; me with my annual Steiff Christmas ornament.

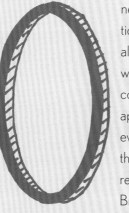

ROOFTOP PIG ROAST

A TEXAS TRADITION WITH A
VIEW OF THE BIG APPLE

O ne thing I've learned as a fashion designer is that inspiration can come anytime, from anywhere—and it doesn't always make sense at first. My collections usually start with a single idea that I build out with notions about fabric, color, mood, memories, and pieces of visual inspiration. I approach parties the same way: I can't start planning an event until I have that first spark of inspiration, but once that happens, I run with it—whatever it is—and build the rest of the party around that first idea. So when I visited Brooklyn Grange, a rooftop farm in Queens, New York, I just knew I had to find a way to throw a party there. The unexpected, almost unimaginable combination of a commercial farm on a rooftop surrounded by the most iconic skyline in the world was too special not to share with my friends, and it reminded me why I love living in New York City. I had planned on hosting a benefit for Edible Schoolyard NYC, an organization that brings

THIS PAGE: As everyone who comes to my parties can attest, I'm someone who loves standing (er, dancing) on a table. For this gathering, I chose a cotton dress that would accommodate everything from shopping at the farmers market on my bike to setting places at the table.

food education and locally grown, produce-focused lunch options to underserved public schools, and I realized that this hidden rooftop garden was the perfect location to showcase their work.

This was going to be a large party—bigger than the dinners I host at home—so I needed to think of something good to serve a large crowd. I drew on my memories of Texas pig pickins'—convivial gatherings centered around a roasted pig and lots of sides—and tried to translate the spirit and tastes that I remembered into the vibe of this party: casual, outdoorsy, and very interactive. There would be lots of vegetables, too—perfect for emphasizing the work of Edible Schoolyard NYC, but which could also do double duty as food and table decor. We would start with cocktails while it was still light out, then cruise into the sunset, so everyone would get to enjoy the magical view of the Manhattan skyline in several kinds of light.

Part of the appeal of this location was the challenge of throwing a party here. Brooklyn Grange is a commercial space, so everything—save for one enormous wooden table—had to be brought in and transported to the rooftop. This meant that the menu had to be planned strategically, eliminating as much fussy on-site work as possible. Chef April Bloomfield, a big supporter of the organization, was enlisted to take on the pig prep and came up with a few easy-to-transport side dishes. The same went for the decor—though when your table has a full view of the New York City skyline, how much else do you really need? I relied on Mason jars, old fashioned-looking metal washbasins, lanterns, strings of lights, and gorgeous fresh vegetables to set a casual, food-driven tone.

I asked my daughter's art teacher to draw a pig, which I then printed on craft paper to make the invitations. I used the same image on the place mats, which I also printed on craft paper and secured to the table with thumbtacks.

L BLOOMFIELD WEDNESDAY SEPTEMBER 14th DRINKS + SUNSET VIEWS 6:30PM DINNER 7PM DINNER AT BROOKLYN GRANGE LOCAL AT BROOKLYN GRANGE S

OPPOSITE: I used late-summer garlic flowers from the Greenmarket to accentuate the un-citylike atmosphere of this gathering, and tied them together with pieces of twine so they could stand upright in the Mason jars. I alternated the jars with metal lanterns in which we placed tea lights. These plus a few strings of twinkling lights and the city skyline were all the light we needed after the sun went down.

THIS PAGE: Brooklyn Grange is a commercial space, so we had to bring every-thing—except the long wooden table—up to the roof ourselves. This was our mandate for unfussy decor. Centerpieces and table decorations came from the Union Square Greenmarket, my favorite place to shop in the city. Instead of vases, we went cheap and cheerful with metal washbasins and Mason jars, which I got from Home Depot.

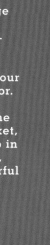

16

The people from Brooklyn Grange were great—they basically gave us free rein to do whatever we wanted—but their one rule/warning was that nothing could fly off the roof, hence the thumbtacks and vegetables! Radishes, carrots, and spring onions added necessary weight to each table setting, as well as bright shots of color—and also nicely referenced the work of Edible Schoolyard NYC.

THINKING OUTSIDE THE HOME

TIPS FOR PARTIES IN UNUSUAL PLACES

Open your mind to unexpected spaces. I've thrown birthday scavenger hunts in public parks for my kids and hosted a mini parade with a mariachi band on my block—I've even thrown a party in the New York City subway! With a little planning, a pop-up party in a parking lot, with decorations strung between lampposts and music blaring from a car window, can be more fun than a regular weekend get-together at home.

Never ask permission. Beg forgiveness later.

Feel free to under-plan one aspect of a party in order to concentrate on others. In this case, logistics took over the bulk of the planning, but once guests were on the roof, the backdrop of the city skyline was pretty much all the decor we needed.

Delicious food doesn't equal fancy food. Good seasonal produce is always your secret weapon.

When you entertain outdoors, you have to cede some of the control that you have in your home. Embrace the unpredictable.

20

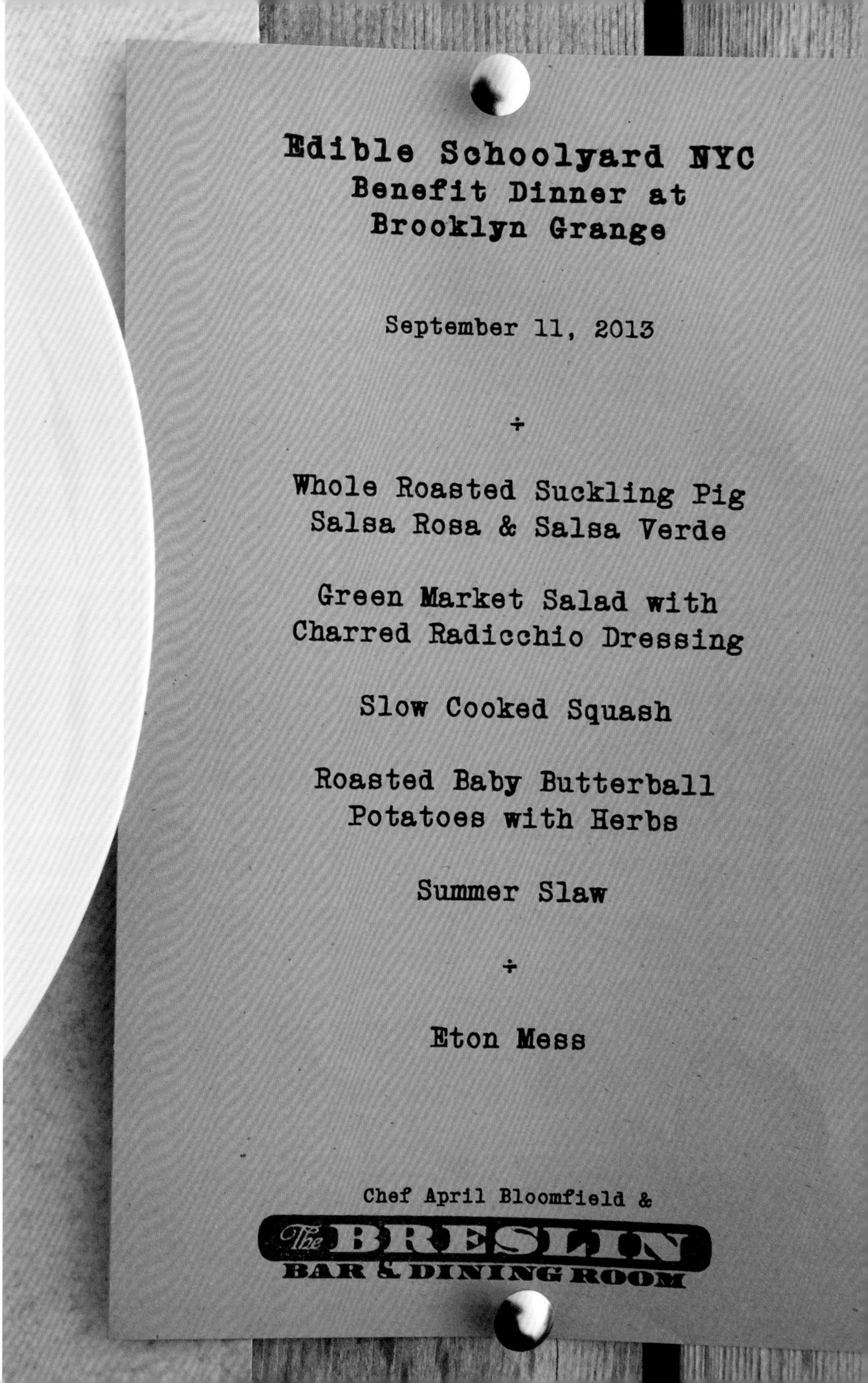

Edible Schoolyard NYC
Benefit Dinner at
Brooklyn Grange

September 11, 2013

✝

Whole Roasted Suckling Pig
Salsa Rosa & Salsa Verde

Green Market Salad with
Charred Radicchio Dressing

Slow Cooked Squash

Roasted Baby Butterball
Potatoes with Herbs

Summer Slaw

✝

Eton Mess

Chef April Bloomfield &

The BRESLIN
BAR & DINING ROOM

Since the food was prepared off-site and brought up to the roof, we served everything all at once, family-style, which fit with the tone of this big, casual gathering. We hosted about fifty people at this dinner, a great number to enjoy a whole roasted pig.

BRANDON'S MARGARITA

The key to a great margarita is good lime juice, the fresher the better—there really is no substitute. Whenever you can, try to squeeze the lime just before you start mixing the drinks.

Serves 8

INGREDIENTS

4 cups good-quality tequila	⅓ cup honey, plus more as needed
2 cups Cointreau	Kosher salt
2 cups fresh lime juice	Ice cubes

In a pitcher, combine the tequila, Cointreau, lime juice, and honey and stir to dissolve the honey. Add additional honey to sweeten, if desired. Drizzle more honey on a small plate. On a separate small plate, pour a layer of salt to a thickness of ⅛ inch. Dip the rims of 8 tumblers into the honey, allowing any excess to drip off, then dip the rims very lightly into the salt. Put a large amount of ice in each tumbler, fill halfway with the margarita, and serve.

VIVA TEQUILA

I n my experience, there's nothing like tequila to get guests enthusiastically on board with whatever crazy concept I'm trying to pull off, so margaritas, which we mixed at home before leaving for the rooftop, were the drink of the evening. Being from Texas, margaritas frequently make appearances at the parties I throw, and we often riff on our basic recipe (above, right) by infusing them with seasonal ingredients: strawberry in the spring; watermelon-jalapeno in the summer; pomegranate or ginger in the fall; and spicy grapefruit or blood orange in winter. My favorite trick is using a little bit of honey to salt each rim.

The salads and side dishes were as simple as can be—just a few quick, seasonal preparations of greens, potatoes, and squash, plus a late-summer slaw—all of which could be made in advance and served at room temperature.

MARINATED OLIVES

Serves 8

INGREDIENTS
2 cups pitted large green olives, drained
½ cup extra virgin olive oil
2 tablespoons chopped fresh parsley
1 tablespoon grated lemon zest
Juice of one lemon
2 teaspoons fennel seed
2 teaspoons fresh thyme leaves
Pepper

In a medium bowl, toss together olives, oil, parsley, lemon zest and juice, fennel and thyme; season with pepper. Let marinate at room temperature 1 hour (or cover and refrigerate, up to 1 week).

For a hostess, being outdoors in a place like a park, public garden, or rooftop means ceding much of the control that you have when you entertain at home. There's no air-conditioning to moderate the temperature, no switch that can be flipped to adjust the lighting. But I find that there's magic in commandeering a gathering in unexpected places—after all, if you're in an unpredictable place, you're pretty much guaranteed a one-of-a-kind party, which is always the best kind anyway.

COUPLES' COOK-OFF
A POTLUCK WITH PRIZES

love to cook, and I love a competition. As anyone who knows me can attest, I've never played a game in which I didn't try my hardest to win (and not always graciously). During the fall when I was looking for inspiration for a weeknight dinner party, I thought, why not try and combine these two passions into a single evening? The resulting gathering was a couples' cook-off that showcased the attendees' skills as well as the season's great produce, and it turned out to be the perfect recipe for a delicious, hilarious, competition-spiked autumn evening.

I'd hosted several game nights in the past, but I chose a cook-off this time because I thought it was a perfect way to get couples invested in the meal and to add an extra element of challenge-driven fun. This also helped me determine the guest list. I needed people competitive enough to get into the spirit and pull out all the stops with their creativity, people who weren't intimidated by putting in time in the kitchen. (Only homemade food was allowed!) I

wanted enough dishes for a real competition, but not so many that it would be impossible to remember each one. I settled on a total of five couples, plus three judges who I recruited from among my friends: a professional cook who had been on *Top Chef*, a magazine editor, and a mixologist.

chose potpies because of the range of possibilities they offer and because they fit with the season. But tacos, soups, stews, gratins—basically any category of food that can be filled or prepared with a range of ingredients—would work too. For the invitation, I created a cooking-themed tableau in autumnal colors with a saucepot, whisk, and vegetables. The dress code for this party was "dress to impress . . . both you and your potpie," to emphasize the importance of presentation.

We held the dinner on a Wednesday evening. Wednesday is the biggest and best day at Manhattan's Union Square Greenmarket and when I do most of my shopping. The morning of the dinner, I biked to the market and filled up my baskets with a cornucopia of colorful autumn produce that later made its way into pies, canapés, and table decor.

AMBITION SHALLOT

Shiitake 12.7/lb.

french breakfast radishes $2.50

I bought almost everything I needed for the party in a single trip to the farmers market. Though I shop here year-round, fall is a particularly exciting time: everything is at its most colorful and flavorful, and the stands are bursting with vegetables, gourds, herbs, and flowers.

When I'm shopping for a party, I ride to the Greenmarket on my cargo bike, which has enough room (usually) for all of my purchases, as well as a little passenger!

I'm always
looking for ways
to set a table
with something
other than
flowers, and fall
vegetables, with
their rich colors
and interesting
textures and
shapes, make
great decorations
for a hearty
autumn meal.

Though the atmosphere was casual, the game most definitely was not. We started off with drinks and canapés while waiting for all the guests to arrive. While the contestants sat down for a salad course, the judges went to work, tasting each potpie and scoring it on presentation, taste, and originality. Then the guests had a chance to taste the competition for themselves as the rankings were announced. I came up with playful names and silly prizes for every couple, from first place ("Winner Winner Chicken Dinner"—a set of herb crowns) to fifth place ("Skip the dinner and go straight to a movie"—boxes of movie-theater candy).

This party perfectly expresses my philosophy that you don't need an occasion to create your own fun. The theme, the contest, and the seasonality came together in a single party simply because I wanted them to. I found that my guests were more than happy to break out of their weeknight routines and bring their all for something a little silly and unexpected.

And the winner? Do you have to ask? It was my party, after all. . . . This evening was about good food, good friends, a good competition, and enjoying the season, but don't think for a second that my eye wasn't on the prize.

Planning out the seating might seem fussy, but having everyone know where to sit actually makes things more comfortable for guests and smooths an often awkward dinner-party moment. If you've got some basic supplies on hand, place cards take only a few minutes to throw together. I keep plenty of metallic pens, ribbons, and thick craft paper at home and save extra card stock from the Christmas cards we make every year, so I can whip up a set of place cards in a few minutes whenever I need them.

224 West 30th Street, 14th floor, New York, New York 10001
tel +1 212 947 9204 fax +1 212 564 8458 www.lelarose.com

OCTOBER 30TH

CookOff MENU

COCKTAILS

- SPICED APPLE SNAP

CANAPES (DECONSTRUCTED POT PIE)

- RUSTIC LOAF FROM SULLIVAN STREET
- DEVILED QUAIL EGGS + CAVIAR
- MUSHROOM TOAST
- ASSORTED CHEESES: SOTTO CENERE, MANCHEGO, CAMEMBERT

SALAD COURSE

- RIBBONED KALE W/ SHAVED APPLES + P

DESSERT

- HONEY + SAGE ICE CREAM
- SUGAR PUFFS ROLLED IN ORANGE S
- CHOCOLATE SAUCE

LEFT: I rounded out the selection of potpies with a salad, and made a few canapés for people to nibble on as other guests arrived. The salad was an improvised mélange from the greenmarket—kale ribbons, Gala apples, and some cheese and nuts I had on hand. FOLLOWING SPREAD, LEFT: The canapés I prepared were light and simple—a chic version of deviled eggs made with quail eggs and caviar, little mushroom toasts, and a cheese plate—because I needed people's stomachs ready to sample all entries in the competition.

OPPOSITE: The evening's cocktails were as seasonally driven as the rest of the food and decor. We served one cocktail with apple cider and Calvados and one with pumpkin.

SPICED APPLE SNAP

For ease, the ingredients in this festive fall drink are mixed in a pitcher, then shaken just before serving. Snap liqueur is an artisanal spirit flavored with a variety of ingredients including blackstrap molasses, ginger, cloves, nutmeg, cinnamon, and rooibos tea. It's available at fine liquor stores.

Serves 8

INGREDIENTS

Cider Syrup
3 cinnamon sticks, broken in half

4 whole cloves

4 star anise

3 whole allspice berries

½ teaspoon ground mace

1 quart apple cider

Cocktail
2 cups hard cider

1 cup fresh lemon juice

1 cup Snap liqueur

1 cup Calvados or Armagnac

Ice cubes

8 lemon twists, for garnish

For the Cider Syrup: Combine the spices in a spice grinder and pulse on and off until coarsely ground. Pour the cider into a large wide pot; add the ground spices and bring to a boil over high heat. Simmer until reduced to about 1 cup (the consistency should resemble maple syrup), about 45 minutes to 1 hour. Let the syrup cool completely. (The cider syrup can be made up to 1 month ahead; pour into a bottle or jar, then cover and refrigerate until ready to use.)

For the Cocktail: In a medium pitcher, combine the cider, lemon juice, cider syrup, Snap liqueur, and Calvados for the cocktail base. (The cocktail base can be made 1 hour ahead. Cover and keep at cool room temperature.)

For each drink, measure ¾ cup of the cocktail base into a shaker and fill with ice. Shake vigorously. Pour the drink into a rocks glass, along with the ice from the shaker. Garnish with a lemon twist.

TARTE DE TRIXIE
(RABBIT POTPIE)

*This recipe calls for cooked rabbit. Use whatever
cooking technique you prefer (sous vide, roast, or braise).
Chicken thighs can be substituted for the rabbit.*

Serves 8–10

INGREDIENTS
Pastry Crust
3 cups plus 2 tablespoons all-purpose flour
1 cup (2 sticks) plus 5 tablespoons unsalted butter,
chilled, cut into 1-inch pieces
1 teaspoon kosher salt
⅔ cup ice water

Filling
8 ounces haricots verts or other slender green beans
16 pearl onions
10 fingerling potatoes

As a fashion designer, I'm always focused on presentation and detailing, whether it be on a dress or in a dish I'm serving. A potpie is a terrific canvas for creative details as well as delicious combinations of flavors. The embroidery on this blouse (left) was the inspiration for the button-like lattice decoration I made on the crust of my pie.

8 tablespoons (1 stick) unsalted butter

1 pound sliced mushrooms

Salt and freshly ground black pepper

2 tablespoons olive oil

3 parsnips, peeled and cut into small dice

5 carrots, peeled and cut into small dice

1 (3-pound) whole rabbit, cut into pieces, cooked, skin removed, cut into medium dice

⅓ cup all-purpose flour

3½ cups chicken stock or low-sodium broth, hot

1 cup heavy cream

1 cup crème fraîche

¼ cup Dijon mustard

1 tablespoon finely chopped fresh tarragon

2 teaspoons finely chopped fresh thyme

1 egg, beaten

For the Pastry Crust: Place the flour in a bowl of a food processor; add the butter and salt and cut it in using on/off turns until the butter is reduced to pea-size pieces. Slowly pour the ice water through the feed tube of the food processor and pulse until the dough just starts to come together in a ball (you should still see some small bits of butter in the dough). Turn the dough out onto a floured work surface and divide into two equal-size balls. Press each ball into a disc about 1 inch thick. Wrap each disc in plastic wrap and refrigerate for at least 4 hours, or overnight.

For the Filling: Cook the haricots verts in a large saucepan of boiling water for 1 minute. Using tongs, transfer the haricots verts to a bowl of ice water to cool quickly, about 2 minutes. Using tongs, transfer the haricots verts to paper towels to drain. Halve the haricots verts crosswise.

Return the water in the pan to a boil; add the pearl onions and boil for 1 minute. Using a slotted spoon, transfer the onions to the bowl of ice water to cool quickly, about 2 minutes. Drain and peel the onions.

Return the water in the pan to a boil; add the potatoes and boil gently until just tender and a skewer easily pierces the centers, about 10 minutes. Drain the potatoes and let cool, then cut into ¼-inch-thick rounds.

Melt 2 tablespoons of the butter in heavy large skillet over medium-high heat. Add the mushrooms and sauté, stirring often, until golden brown, about 15 minutes. Season with salt and pepper. Transfer the mushrooms to a large bowl and set aside. Heat the olive oil in the same skillet over high heat. Add the pearl onions and sauté until beginning to soften, about 5 minutes. Add the parsnips, carrots, and potatoes and sauté the vegetables until golden brown, about 15 minutes. Add the diced rabbit to the vegetable mixture. (The filling can be made to this point 1 day ahead. Cover and refrigerate until ready to use.)

Melt the remaining 6 tablespoons butter in a heavy medium saucepan over medium heat. Add the flour and cook for 2 to 3 minutes, whisking continuously. Add the stock and bring to a boil, whisking until smooth. Add the cream and crème fraîche; cook, whisking continuously, until the sauce thickens enough to coat the back of a spoon, 3 to 4 minutes. Whisk in the mustard, tarragon, and thyme. Season the sauce with salt and pepper. Let the sauce cool slightly. Pour the sauce over the vegetable-rabbit mixture and mix gently to combine. Season with salt and pepper.

Preheat the oven to 400°F.

Transfer the filling to a 3-inch deep, 9- to 10-inch round ovenproof earthenware dish to within ½ inch from the top edge.

Roll out 1 dough disc on a floured surface to about ⅛-inch thickness. Brush the beaten egg onto the rim and about halfway down the outside of the baking dish to hold the crust in place while baking. Place the rolled pastry over the filling, allowing about 2 inches to drape over the edges. Press into place to adhere to the dish, then cut away any excess dough and reserve for decorations. Brush the entire crust with beaten egg; cut eight small slits in the top for steam to escape.

Roll the dough trimmings and second dough piece and form into small balls or other decorative shapes and attach to the crust. Brush the decorations with more egg.

Place the baking dish on a rimmed baking sheet. Bake until the crust is nicely browned and the sauce bubbles thickly through the vents, 30 to 35 minutes. Let cool slightly and serve.

Naturally, coming up with an outfit that fits the theme is one of my favorite parts of the planning process. For this party, I took inspiration from the seasonal touches of the menu and table decor and dressed in a fall palette and made oven mitts to match.

HONEY-SAGE ICE CREAM

I served this with Sugar Puffs, which are small popovers rolled in cinnamon and sugar, and topped it with homemade chocolate sauce.

Serves 8

INGREDIENTS

2 cups whole milk

4 teaspoons cornstarch

1 ½ ounces cream cheese, at room temperature

Pinch of salt

1 ½ cups heavy cream

⅔ cup honey

2 tablespoons light corn syrup

10 fresh sage leaves

Good quality chocolate sauce, for drizzling

Additional fresh sage leaves, for garnish (optional)

Whisk ¼ cup of the milk with the cornstarch in a small bowl until smooth. In another small bowl, mix the cream cheese and salt until smooth. Set both bowls aside.

Combine the cream, honey, corn syrup, and remaining 1 ¾ cups milk in a heavy medium saucepan and bring to a boil. Remove the pan from the heat and whisk in the cornstarch mixture. Bring to a boil over medium-high heat. Continue cooking, whisking continuously, until the mixture thickens slightly, 1 to 2 minutes. Remove from the heat; add the cream cheese mixture and whisk until smooth and lump-free. Add the sage leaves; cover and let steep for 20 to 30 minutes.

Remove and discard the sage leaves. Pour the mixture into a container and refrigerate, uncovered, until cold. (The ice cream base can be made to this point 1 day ahead. Cover and keep refrigerated until ready to use.)

Process the chilled ice cream base in an ice cream maker according to the manufacturer's instructions.

Scoop the ice cream into bowls. Spoon warm chocolate sauce over the ice cream. Garnish with more sage leaves, if desired.

for le judge ♡

for le judge ♡

for le ju

SORACHI ACE

SORACHI ACE

SORACHI ACE

LOBSTER
Potted Pie...

I've always thought that challenges—intentional ones—are a great way to spice up a dinner party. They give everyone a common purpose for being there and force some creativity and spiritedness from the guests (and give me an outlet to channel my competitive nature). I made sure the judges took their roles seriously, but to keep the tone playful, I came up with jokey names and prizes for each couple, from first to fifth place. When the rankings were announced, we were all laughing so hard that not even the fifth-place couple—who received boxes of candy and a note suggesting that next time they skip making dinner and catch a movie instead—seemed to mind.

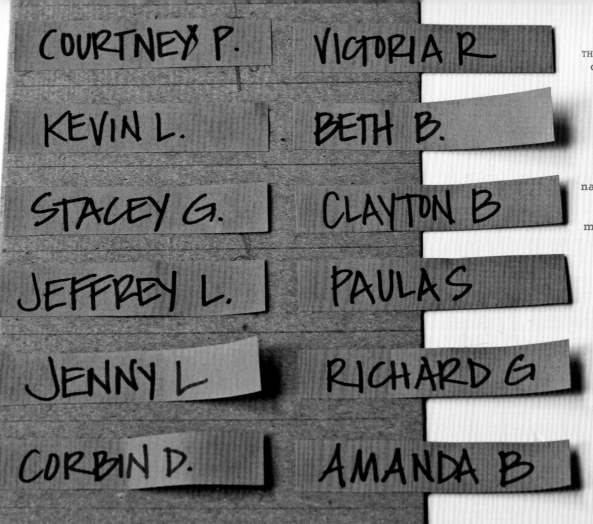

COURTNEY P.   VICTORIA R

KEVIN L.   BETH B.

STACEY G.   CLAYTON B

JEFFREY L.   PAULA S

JENNY L   RICHARD G

CORBIN D.   AMANDA B

HEALTHY COMPETITION
TIPS FOR A TASTY COOK-OFF

Fall is a great time of year for a sit-down dinner party with friends. The produce is colorful and vibrant, guests are in the mood for hearty home-cooked meals, and friends are excited to see one another after summer vacations.

Competition is a great way to spice up a gathering. And I firmly believe that if you're going to have a competition, you need to have prizes. And judges.

A cook-off is an easy party to throw together on a weeknight, because everyone helps with the meal.

Guests cannot survive on potpies alone. No matter what dish you choose for your cook-off, round it out with a salad or side. But don't go crazy with the hors d'oeuvres—you want people to save room for the main event.

The invitation said "dress to impress." This was a challenge, not a suggestion. My secret weapon: matching my oven mitts to my outfit.

WHITE CHRISTMAS
A DRESSED-UP HOLIDAY DINNER

When it comes to entertaining, my natural inclination is to ignore what convention or the calendar dictates and follow my whims toward less expected, more idiosyncratic celebrations. But not at Christmas.

I treasure my Christmas memories, many of them based around childhood traditions that I now continue with my own family. As a little girl, I was given a Steiff animal every year to use as a Christmas ornament, and today I add to my childhood menagerie by buying Steiff animals for my own children. Another one of my favorite holiday traditions was the string gift. On Christmas morning, after we had opened everything else, our mother would reveal one final present: a tiny box with the end of a string in it. We would follow the string around the house until it led us to the last surprise, which was always something for the whole family. I now do this every year with my kids, and as it was when I was a child, the string gift is always the most anticipated moment of the day.

My annual Christmas gathering is another tradition, one that is all my own. This is the fanciest, most occasion-centric event I throw, and unlike many of my parties, it embraces traditional trappings of the holiday: gift giving, festive food and drink, and a decorated tree. But just because it is an annual party doesn't mean I follow the same template year after year. I like to find new themes, new colors, and new inspirations for each meal.

If, come December, you grow weary of the chaos of competing cocktail parties, this is a dinner for you. In fact, the thing I love most about my Christmas gathering—and what makes it stand out among each year's slew of holiday-season parties—is its formality. This is a sit-down dinner, no drop-ins allowed. We invite our closest friends, who know that they will be attending a complete Christmas evening, including festive cocktails; a delicious, decadent meal; and gift opening. For me, it's an occasion to pull out all the stops with elegance and prepare lavish courses, full of special ingredients that I dream up weeks before. And I promise that, as a hostess, this kind of entertaining is infinitely more enjoyable than the type where guests are constantly coming in and out, and where you spend the entire night saying hello and good-bye and monitoring the level of food and drink.

I choose a different theme for every Christmas party so that each one has its own magic. This year, I decided on the color white, in homage to the classic film *White Christmas* and the name of my beloved TriBeCa block. This also allowed me to work in a "white elephant" gift exchange, and it set the tone for an elegant dress code: winter white or sparkling silver. For the invitation, I created a winter wonderland on craft paper with miniature Christmas trees sprinkled with fake snow and wrote the information in a Christmasy script. My son, Grey, started a company called Cool Bike Lights, which are little lights he makes to wrap through your bike spokes. I borrowed a string of those lights for my tableau and wove them around the trees. Then I took a picture to send to the invitees.

61

Nothing makes a guest feel more welcome than a thoughtful touch that gets them smiling—especially right as they are entering your home. At this party, two waiters stood outside our apartment to greet guests with sparklers, which immediately put everyone in the mood for a lively evening. When I throw parties at home, I try to think of some fun, new way to welcome guests to the party. The moment when a guest arrives is so important: it's the transition into the world of your party, and it's the perfect time to surround them with the theme of the evening. The gesture can be as lavish or playful as you like— even an unexpected piece of decoration in the entry will help them get in the mood for whatever you've got in store.

Formal does not need to mean stuffy; I always find a way to work in some on-theme, off-kilter touches, even on my fanciest tables. I used my nicest china, silver, and crystal for this dinner but kept it loose by mixing in different shapes and patterns as well as silver ornament napkin rings and handmade place cards. Everything was white and silver in keeping with the theme, which also made the table look appropriately put together. By playing with texture, shape, pattern, and shades of color, you can create a look that is sophisticated but still has some fun and originality in it.

DRESSY DINNERS DONE EASY

Keep the guest list small: Don't invite more people than can comfortably eat in your home and that you feel able to cook for.

Match your menu: If your party has a theme, use that to guide everything that you serve, from cocktails through dessert.

State your intentions clearly: Use the word "dinner" rather than "party," and give people a specific hour (rather than a range of times) to discourage drop-ins. And don't forget to ask for an RSVP.

Make menu cards: Handwritten menus communicate that your guests are in for something special. A well-named signature cocktail can also go a long way in setting a formal (and fun) tone.

Don't try anything new: Seated dinners are not the time to experiment with new recipes. Stick with dishes that you have made before and you will be less stressed before and during the party.

Think ahead: Make as much ahead of time as possible to cut down on last-minute surprises. Many recipes (including the ones in this book) tell you what can be made in advance.

RUM FLIP

Use best-quality aged rum in this holiday favorite and shake each drink individually.

Serves 8

INGREDIENTS
1 ½ cups aged rum
8 large eggs
8 tablespoons heavy cream
8 rounded teaspoons sugar
Ice cubes

For each drink, combine 3 tablespoons rum, 1 egg, 1 tablespoon cream, and 1 rounded teaspoon sugar in a cocktail shaker. Add about 1 cup ice cubes and shake vigorously until frothy, about 20 seconds. Strain the drink into a coupe glass and serve.

ACORN SQUASH SALAD
WITH WINTER RADISHES, WHITE MISO
VINAIGRETTE, AND PUMPKIN SEEDS

Serves 8

INGREDIENTS

2 medium acorn squash

Sea salt and freshly ground black pepper

4 fresh thyme sprigs

2 tablespoons plus 1 cup olive oil

2 tablespoons unsalted butter

4 heads garlic, cloves separated and peeled

1 large onion, peeled and roughly chopped

6 ounces white miso

¼ cup apple cider vinegar

2 tablespoons maple syrup

3 or 4 radishes, thinly sliced with a mandoline or knife

¼ cup salted pumpkin seeds, toasted

2 teaspoons Szechuan or pink peppercorns*

Preheat the oven to 350°F.

Rinse the squash carefully to remove any dirt from the skin. Using a heavy large knife, split the squash in half and scoop out the seeds. Pat the squash dry with a paper towel. Place the squash cut-side up on a rimmed baking sheet. Season the inside of the squash with salt and black pepper. Divide the thyme sprigs, 2 tablespoons of the olive oil, and the butter between the cavities. Cover with aluminum foil and roast until the flesh is tender but still has some texture, about 1 hour. Uncover and let the squash cool to room temperature.

While the squash is cooking, heat the remaining 1 cup oil in a heavy medium saucepan over low heat. Add the garlic and cook until it is tender and sweet, about 20 minutes. Strain the garlic oil into a heavy large saucepan; reserve the garlic. Add the onion to the garlic oil and cook over low heat, stirring occasionally, until tender, about 20 minutes. Let the onion mixture cool, then transfer it to a blender. Add the reserved garlic and puree.

Place the miso in a large bowl and slowly whisk in the onion-garlic puree. Add the vinegar and maple syrup; whisk to combine. Season the dressing with salt and black pepper.

Slice the squash into half-moons, about ½ inch thick. Arrange the squash on plates. Top with thin slices of radish and drizzle with the miso vinaigrette. Garnish with pumpkin seeds. Sprinkle with sea salt and cracked Szechuan pepper.

Szechuan pepper is available at specialty foods stores.

70

Though I usually try to tailor my menus to the party theme, in this case, all-white food seemed . . . well, unappetizing, both creatively and taste-wise. Instead, I mixed some seasonal ingredients in with the theme, such as the elegant acorn squash crowns and white miso vinaigrette in this salad. When I host a meal, I like to treat my guests to unusual dishes, so for the main course, I served partridge with quince and ginger.

AUNT BETTY'S DEVIL'S FOOD CAKE WITH DIVINITY ICING

If you are adding notes or fortunes, individually wrap the notes in waxed paper or parchment paper and include a string if you want guests to be able to pull them out.

Serves 10 to 12

INGREDIENTS
Cake

1 cup sifted cake flour

¾ cup all-purpose flour

1 teaspoon baking soda

¼ teaspoon salt

9 tablespoons unsalted butter, at room temperature

¾ cup granulated sugar

½ cup packed light brown sugar

1 ounce unsweetened chocolate, melted

1 teaspoon pure vanilla extract

2 large eggs

1 cup buttermilk

Icing

2 cups granulated sugar

5 large egg whites, room temperature

Pinch of salt

1 teaspoon pure vanilla extract

2 to 3 teaspoons silver glitter dust, for garnish*

For the Cake: Preheat the oven to 350°F. Grease and flour two 8-inch round cake pans.

In a medium bowl, sift together both flours, the baking soda, and the salt two to three times; set aside. In a large bowl using a hand mixer, cream the butter and sugars together until light and fluffy, about 5 minutes. Add the melted chocolate and vanilla and beat to blend. Add the eggs one at a time, beating quickly. Alternately add the flour mixture and the buttermilk as quickly as possible; do not overbeat. Divide the batter between the prepared cake pans and place wrapped fortunes, if using, equidistant from each other in one cake pan only (this will become your top layer). Bake the cakes until a tester inserted into the center comes out clean, 25 to 30 minutes. Let the cakes cool in the pans on a wire rack.

For the Icing: Bring 1 cup water to a boil in a heavy medium saucepan. Reduce the heat to low; add the sugar and stir until it has dissolved. Increase the heat to medium-high and boil without stirring until the syrup spins a heavy thread or registers 230 to 235°F on a candy thermometer, 10 to 15 minutes.

While the syrup boils, beat the egg whites and a pinch of salt in a large, clean bowl until stiff and dry.

Remove the sugar syrup from the heat. Slowly and very carefully, stream the syrup into the stiff egg whites while beating on medium speed, stopping often to scrape down the sides of the bowl. Then, add the vanilla and beat on high speed until very stiff.

Place the bottom cake layer (the layer without the fortunes) on a platter. Ice and top with second cake layer. Spread the remaining icing over the top and sides of cake, creating peaks. If using glitter dust, dip the tip of a small knife into the dust. Point the knife toward the cake, about 2 inches away. Lightly blow the dust and it will spread evenly on the cake. Repeat where glitter dust is desired. (The cake can be made 8 hours ahead. Let the cake stand at room temperature until ready to serve.)

*Available at cake and candy supply stores.

THE ICING ON THE CAKE

love baking little things into cakes. It's fun for any party, but it's especially nice at Christmas, when gifts and surprises are part of the spirit of the holiday. You can bake almost anything into a cake that can withstand the heat of an oven. (I have used loose change, tiny dollhouse objects, and even little rattles for a baby shower.) I always wrap what I bake into cakes in bits of wax paper. At this party, the cake became part of the white elephant gift exchange. Instead of having guests draw numbers, I baked little cards with numbers written on them into the cake. (I attached string to the cards so people could pull them out without getting their fingers messy, though you can leave the strings out if you want the bake-ins to be a surprise—just warn people not to bite down too hard.) Dessert then flowed naturally into the post-meal entertainment, as guests learned of their order in the gift draw by the number they received in their slice of cake. We played by traditional white elephant (or as it's sometimes known, Yankee swap) rules: on his or her turn, each guest has the option of picking a gift from the pile or stealing the gift from the person who picked before them. (The person who picks first has the option of stealing from the person who picks last.)

SPIN-A-YARN
SUNDAY SUPPER
A CASUAL WEEKEND GET-TOGETHER

f I had to pick my favorite kind of meal, I'd choose a leisurely Sunday supper. I like them because they're comforting and connote a gathering of friends and family—casual, cheerful, and homey. Given the day of the week, I like to use the occasion to connect with friends and neighbors in a different way than I would at a big dinner party or on a lively night out on the town.

The idea behind this supper came from my children. They are always asking to hear about where they came from, the people that came before them, and what we were like as kids. Their quest for stories made me realize how much I like to learn about other people's backgrounds and upbringings, so I decided to put together a meal around the idea of spinning a yarn and asked my guests to bring a favorite tale to tell.

love to play with words and work them into a theme that I then carry through the food and decor. For this invitation, I used brightly colored yarn and metallic paper to spell out the information and then gathered a bunch of colored spools to make a tableau, took a picture of it, and e-mailed it out. On the table, I used pieces of black-and-white mottled yarn to make the shape of each guest's first initial on top of his or her plate in lieu of place cards. The food and drink were things that either had a story behind them or alluded to the past: Old-Fashioneds, my grandfather's buttermilk pralines (made from a recipe that he invented to try to re-create ones that my grandparents tasted on a trip to San Antonio in the 1940s), and a seafood gumbo that my came from my grandmother's housekeeper. To start, I served oysters three ways and bite-size cubes of polenta with prosciutto, held together with mother-of-pearl pushpins as a riff on pearls of wisdom. My guests—a few close friends who live in the neighborhood—arrived in the late afternoon, and we sipped on cocktails while the gumbo simmered. Then we uncorked the wine, served the meal, and soon enough, the stories started flowing!

THE 3 C'S: COMFORT, COLOR, AND CREATIVITY

A Sunday supper should be casual and cozy, a time to catch up with friends before the beginning of a new week. Instead of my long dining table, I served supper on our low cocktail table in the living room. Everyone kicked off their shoes and sat on the floor, which encouraged a comfortable, relaxed mood. I decorated the table with things that I picked up from around the house. A mix of votives and gray candles in brass candlesticks created a warm atmosphere and a nice variety of sizes and shapes on the table. Branches and colorful fruit are a mainstay of my tabletop decor—here, I used persimmons and clementines. The plates were in colors that contrasted with the felted wool tablecloth we were eating on. Having a colorful table is a great trick for entertaining—it automatically lends a visual pop to whatever look you are putting together. I used gold flatware instead of silver to keep the look very warm and wrapped parts of the branches with gold thread to give them a little shimmer and to emphasize the idea of spinning a yarn.

OLD-FASHIONED

Big ice cubes melt slowly in this old-school Kentucky cocktail. Look for extra-large silicone ice cube molds at cookware and cocktail stores.

Serves 8

INGREDIENTS
8 teaspoons sugar
16 dashes Angostura bitters
2 cups rye or bourbon whiskey

Ice, preferably eight
2-inch cubes
8 orange twists,
for garnish

For each drink: Measure 1 teaspoon sugar into an old-fashioned glass. Moisten the sugar with 2 drops of bitters. Top with ¼ cup rye or bourbon and add ice. Rub an orange twist around the rim of the glass, add it to the drink, and serve.

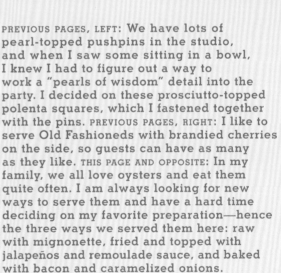

PREVIOUS PAGES, LEFT: We have lots of pearl-topped pushpins in the studio, and when I saw some sitting in a bowl, I knew I had to figure out a way to work a "pearls of wisdom" detail into the party. I decided on these prosciutto-topped polenta squares, which I fastened together with the pins. PREVIOUS PAGES, RIGHT: I like to serve Old Fashioneds with brandied cherries on the side, so guests can have as many as they like. THIS PAGE AND OPPOSITE: In my family, we all love oysters and eat them quite often. I am always looking for new ways to serve them and have a hard time deciding on my favorite preparation—hence the three ways we served them here: raw with mignonette, fried and topped with jalapeños and remoulade sauce, and baked with bacon and caramelized onions.

GRILLED PRAWN, ANDOUILLE SAUSAGE, AND CRABMEAT GUMBO

The oven-baked method of making the roux explained here is much simpler than the traditional method of cooking the flour on the stovetop—and produces far fewer burn injuries. This recipe calls for best quality seafood stock. You can either make your own or buy the best quality. A richly flavored stock adds a great flavor to gumbo. This is important so as to not break the roux.

Serves 8

INGREDIENTS

1 ½ cups all-purpose flour

1 ½ cups vegetable oil

1 large onion, peeled and chopped

3 celery stalks, chopped

2 medium green bell peppers, stemmed, seeded, and chopped

2 jalapeño peppers, stemmed, seeded, and finely chopped

2 garlic cloves, minced

6 cups best quality seafood stock, plus more as needed, warm or at room temperature

1 tablespoon salt

1 ½ teaspoons paprika

1 ½ teaspoons filé powder

1 ½ teaspoons chili powder

2 teaspoons freshly ground black pepper

2 tablespoons grapeseed oil or other neutral oil

1 pound andouille sausage, cut into 1-inch-thick slices

1 pound crab claw meat, carefully picked over for shells

8 large prawns, shelled on body only with heads and tails left on

4 cups cooked white or brown rice

8 fresh parsley sprigs, for garnish

Hot sauce, for serving (optional)

Preheat the oven to 350°F.

In a 5- or 6-quart cast-iron Dutch oven, whisk together the flour and vegetable oil. You don't want any lumps of flour left, so whisk well. Place the Dutch oven on the middle shelf of the oven, uncovered, and bake for 1 ½ hours. Stir the roux three or four times while it is cooking. The roux is done when it is the color of an old penny. Do not let it burn, as burnt roux will ruin the taste of the gumbo.

Remove the pot from the oven and set it on the stovetop over medium heat. (The roux can be made ahead of time and stored in the refrigerator in an airtight container for up to 1 month. It will need to be gently heated over medium heat before adding anything to it.)

Carefully add the onion, celery, bell peppers, jalapeños, and garlic (you don't want to burn yourself on the hot roux). Mix to fully coat the vegetables in the roux. Raise the heat to medium-high and cook, stirring frequently, until the onions start to turn translucent and the vegetables have softened, 10 to 12 minutes.

Once the vegetables have softened, add the seafood stock and stir to combine.

Add the salt, paprika, filé powder, chili powder, and black pepper. Stir to combine. Bring to a boil and cook for 10 minutes, then reduce the heat to maintain a simmer and cover the pot with a tight-fitting lid. Let simmer for 45 minutes to 1 hour. The oil will start separating from the broth and will rise to the top. Skim it off and discard several times over the course of the cooking time. Taste and adjust the seasoning. If the broth has too strong a roux flavor, you can add water or more stock, 1 cup at a time, to even it out.

Add the sausage pieces and crabmeat and simmer for 5 minutes more. (The sausage is already cooked, so it just needs to heat through.)

In a grill pan, heat the grapeseed oil over medium-high heat. When oil is hot, grill the prawns for 3 minutes per side. They will have a bright pink color when done. Set aside.

Spoon ½ cup rice into each of eight individual serving bowls. Ladle in the gumbo to fill the bowls three-quarters of the way. Top each bowl with one grilled prawn and a sprig of parsley to garnish. Serve hot, with hot sauce on the side for those who want to spice it up.

I served the gumbo in a set of Charlotte tins that my mother gave me soon after I moved to New York from Texas. She had visited when I first moved to the city, and we went out for a delicious meal that ended with the most amazing pear Charlotte. She later found these tins and gave them to me as a gift to celebrate my move to the big city. They have accompanied me from apartment to apartment and have been used to serve all kinds of dishes: chili, tortilla soup, and, of course, pear Charlotte!

GRANDJOHN'S BUTTERMILK PRALINE RECIPE

Makes approximately 24 medium pralines

INGREDIENTS
2 cups sugar
¾ cup buttermilk
⅓ cup heavy cream
1 teaspoon baking soda

1 ½ teaspoons pure vanilla extract
3 tablespoons unsalted butter
Pinch of sea salt
1 cup pecans, coarsely chopped

Line a baking sheet with waxed paper.

In a heavy-bottomed pot, combine the sugar, buttermilk, cream, and baking soda. Clip a candy thermometer to the side of the pot and cook over medium-low heat, stirring just enough to keep the mixture from burning, especially as it thickens. Periodically test to see if the mixture is done by lifting the spoon and dropping a couple of drops into a cup of cold water. It is done when the drops form a soft ball in the cold water or the temperature registers 235 to 245°F on the candy thermometer, usually between 15 to 25 minutes.

Remove from the heat and whisk in the vanilla, butter, and salt. Beat until thick and creamy. Quickly add the pecans and stir to incorporate. Drop tablespoonfuls of the mixture onto the prepared baking sheet. Let cool completely before serving.

A portrait of Grandjohn, drawn by his sister Evelyn, my mother's namesake.

EVERYTHING'S COMING UP ROSEY
A PRETTY-IN-PINK BIRTHDAY PARTY

M y mother threw some fabulously creative birthday parties for me and my brother when we were growing up. One of my favorites was one she did for my brother, where she hired a naturalist from the local college to lead us on a nature walk. We set out in the woods with our friends and spent the afternoon looking for interesting critters and trying to catch butterflies in the little nets we had been given. After the party, we were allowed to keep our butterfly nets and critter jars. I could hardly wait to go on my next adventure.

All of the birthday parties of my childhood were centered around an activity where we learned to make or do something. My mother was DIY well before the acronym became popular. She passed this quality on to me, in part, by including my brother and me in the planning for our birthday parties. Together we would come up with creative touches that made each party exciting, different, and tons of fun.

have taken the same approach, and each year, my children and I plan parties for their birthdays inspired by their interests. For my son, we've put on a scavenger hunt and had an O.K. Corral party with a water gun shoot-out held at high noon. My daughter Rosey's parties are usually centered around some kind of craft project with a fashion element. Once, we threw a 1950s sock hop where the girls got to iron homemade decals of poodles (and Norwich terriers, of course) onto skirts I made. Another year, we did a cowgirl-themed party where all of the kids made stick horses and decorated them with fringe and Western trims. These parties are not only enjoyable for us to plan—my kids love brainstorming ideas for their parties and get so excited about the special details we come up with together—but they are also immensely more satisfying (not to mention economical) than renting a venue and hiring entertainment.

The spark of inspiration for this party came from a random thought and a play on words. "Everything's Coming Up Roses," the old show tune from *Gypsy*, couldn't have been a better fit: it gave us a color (pink), a fashion element (roses), and it even had my daughter's name in the title (well, almost). Using the song as a guide, we decided on a pink-themed party where Rosey and her girlfriends would decorate T-shirts and headbands with roses that we

made from old fabric scraps. We decided to hold it in my studio, so we could pull in extra laces, buttons, and scraps of patterns for the girls to decorate with.

The rest of the planning was pretty easy. Everything—the decorations, the food, the dress code for the little guests—had to be pink. I made chicken salad with Pink Lady apples that were served on purple cabbage leaves, pink hard-boiled eggs (I dipped them in beet juice, but food coloring also works), rose-colored peppermint bark, white chocolate-covered strawberries, a rose-petal punch, and a strawberry cake that was decorated with actual roses.

We requested that our guests come "pretty in pink," and they all complied—one of Rosey's friends even donned a platinum pink wig for the entire party! Each girl got to pick a shirt and a headband, and then they sat down at a table I had set up with scissors, glue, and a basket filled with different fabric roses. I gave the girls a general idea of what we were making, but they really created their own pieces. At the end, we hung all the shirts up in the showroom to make the girls feel like fashion designers, and everyone got to look at the special "collection" while they ate and drank.

Kids' birthday parties can be overwhelming and full of store-bought excess. By throwing a party like this—one where the entertainment is a project everyone can do—you set an example for your kids that the best fun comes from imagination and creativity.

Whether this is your first craft project or your umpteenth, as a parent, it's so much fun to watch the delight and excitement of kids when they are making something for themselves.

I bought a stack of plain cotton T-shirts from Zara in pale pink, hot pink, black, and white. Each little girl chose a shirt in her favorite color, and I helped them attach fabric flowers and other decorations with fabric glue. We found plenty of odds and ends in the studio to use, but you can easily buy everything you need—lace, buttons, even fabric flowers— online or at a craft store.

A DREAM COME TRUE

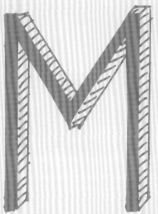

any little girls dream of becoming a fashion designer and love the idea of making their own clothes, and this is a wonderful way to let them experience the joy of creating something pretty that they can keep and wear. The elements of this project—simple cotton T-shirts, buttons, pieces of fabric and lace, and fabric glue—are easy to come by, but they become special when they're used to transform a plain T-shirt or headband into a unique creation. I made the fabric flowers in advance by rolling strips of printed cotton and colorful tulle into circles and fastening the centers with pretty buttons, but you can also buy pre-made fabric flowers at fabric stores and craft stores.

Using real china and silverware makes everything feel more memorable, even at a kids' party. You can pick up interesting pieces at yard sales, thrift stores, and online. I brightened up the tables by placing pink paper flowers into large spools of thread—a nod to the party's setting.

Once you have a theme, it's a lot easier (and more fun) to come up with food and decorations that go with it. Here, the mandate was simple—pink and roses, wherever we could fit them in. We made fuchsia fabric flowers from old lace, which we used as coasters and tied around bags of pink peppermint bark that the girls took home along with their shirts and headbands.

PINK LADY PUNCH

Serves 8

INGREDIENTS
4 cups cranberry juice, chilled
4 cups prepared lemonade, chilled
4 cups ginger ale, chilled
Ice cubes
8 lemon wedges

In a large glass dispenser or punch bowl, combine the cranberry juice, lemonade, and ginger ale. Fill 8 glasses with ice, add punch, and garnish each glass with a lemon wedge.

WHITE CHOCOLATE PEPPERMINT BARK

Makes about 2 pounds

INGREDIENTS
2 pounds white chocolate, cut into ½-inch pieces
12 large candy canes, unwrapped
½ teaspoon pure vanilla extract

Line a baking sheet with parchment paper and set aside.

Place the candy canes in a large resealable plastic bag. Using a mallet or rolling pin, crush the candy into ¼-inch pieces.

Place the white chocolate in the top of a double boiler over simmering water; stir until melted and smooth. Mix the candy cane pieces and vanilla into the chocolate. Remove the chocolate from the heat. Pour the chocolate mixture onto the prepared baking sheet; spread it evenly. Refrigerate until firm, about 30 minutes. Break the bark into pieces. (The bark can be made up to 1 day ahead. Refrigerate in an airtight container for up to 1 week.)

Before the party, Rosey and I walked around our apartment looking for things that fit our theme and could be used for decorations. We found this monkey that I had picked up in a vintage store in Austin and voilà—the perfect touch for our rose-colored table. Before my parties, I always look at what I have at home and see what I can pull in for new and creative purposes. It's a great activity to do with kids; it's fun, and also teaches them to first think about what you can make with what you already have.

STRAWBERRY CAKE WITH PINK ROSES

FAVORITE FAVORS

Coming up with party favors that expand upon the theme can be a fun part of the planning process for a kids' party. At our parties, sometimes the favors are things the guests create themselves during the party (like the shirts and headbands here); other times, it's a small gift that goes with the theme but still emphasizes making, building, or learning. To me, these kinds of favors are a win-win: the coordination with the party makes them feel more special than regular goody bags, and they allow you to avoid candy and plastic toys. Here are a few ideas:

Wild West Party: Fill Mason jars with measured ingredients for Cowboy cookies (made with oats, pecans, and chocolate chips), and attach a recipe around the jar's neck.

Petite Parisian Party: Give a map of Paris along with Eiffel Tower cookie cutters.

Poker Party: Give a deck of cards and instructions for Texas Hold 'Em (our favorite card game) for a kids' poker party.

High-Noon Hoedown: The kids take home the water guns and bandannas they used during the shoot-out.

Sock Hop: Have the girls iron poodle decals onto skirts at the party, and these can double as a favor. Cat-eye sunglasses are an optional bonus item.

Bug Birthday Bash: A bug jar with a guide to insects and butterflies inside is a great gift for a nature-walk party.

FRESH STRAWBERRY CAKE

Serves 10–12

INGREDIENTS
Strawberry Cake
1 pint fresh strawberries, hulled and quartered
3 cups cake flour
4 teaspoons baking powder
½ teaspoon salt
1 cup (2 sticks) unsalted butter, at room temperature
2 cups granulated sugar
4 large eggs, at room temperature
2 teaspoons pure vanilla extract
2 to 4 drops pink food coloring (optional)

Frosting
2 (8-ounce) packages reduced-fat cream cheese, at room temperature
2 cups confectioners' sugar
2 teaspoons pure vanilla extract
4 cups heavy cream, chilled

For the Strawberry Cake: Preheat the oven to 350°F. Grease three 8-inch round cake pans.

Puree enough of the strawberries in a food processor to make 1 ¼ cups smooth puree. Set the puree aside.

Sift together the flour, baking powder, and salt in a bowl and set aside.

In the bowl of a stand mixer fitted with the paddle attachment, beat the butter until light and fluffy, 3 to 5 minutes. Gradually add the granulated sugar and beat until well blended. Reduce the mixer speed to low. Add the eggs one at a time, beating until each is incorporated before adding the next. With the mixer on low speed, beat in one-third of the flour mixture alternately with half of the pureed strawberries. Keep alternating until all the ingredients are just incorporated. Do not overbeat. Fold in the vanilla and food coloring (if using) just until evenly distributed.

Divide the batter evenly among the prepared pans. Bake the cakes until a toothpick inserted into the center comes out clean, 25 to 30 minutes. (The cakes will slightly shrink from the sides and will spring back when lightly touched in the center when done.) Let the cakes cool completely in the pans on wire racks. Run a small sharp knife between the cakes and the pans to loosen the cakes. Turn the cakes out onto wire racks. (The cakes can be made up to 1 day ahead. Cover and set aside at room temperature until ready to use.)

For the Frosting: In the bowl of a stand mixer fitted with the paddle attachment, beat the cream cheese until smooth. Gradually add the confectioners' sugar and beat until light and fluffy. Add the vanilla. Remove the paddle attachment and switch to whisk attachment. Beat the frosting on medium speed for a few seconds. Reduce the mixer speed to low and slowly add the chilled heavy cream. (Tip: cream beats better when well chilled.) Increase the mixer speed to high and beat until the frosting forms stiff peaks.

To Assemble: Place one cake layer on a platter. Spread a layer of frosting evenly over the cake. Top with a layer of chopped strawberries, leaving a ½-inch border from the edge of cake (this prevents the strawberries from spilling out the sides of the cake once it's fully frosted). Spread another layer of frosting over the strawberries, then top with a second cake layer. Repeat the frosting and layering process with the remaining frosting, strawberries, and cake. Cover the entire cake with the remaining frosting.

OLD-FASHIONED
SEWING CIRCLE
A NEW-FASHIONED BRIDAL SHOWER

Bridal showers have always seemed to me like ideal occasions for fun and creativity—my two favorite aspects of parties. Yet so often, I find they follow an unwritten (and uninspired) template. So when one of the women who works in my studio got engaged, I decided to throw her a shower with an extra twist: we'd do it as an old-fashioned sewing circle. In lieu of buying shower gifts, the guests would stitch the couple's initials onto napkins so that the bride-to-be would leave the shower with a one-of-a-kind set of linens.

My inspiration was a black-and-white picture of a sewing circle from the 1940s that I came across when I started brainstorming ideas for this party. I arranged a scene with a bunch of sewing-themed items—spools of thread, measuring tape—on a corkboard. I "wrote" the information in seam tape, took a photo of it, and e-mailed it to guests—my version of an e-vite. The dress code was also the color scheme: old, new, borrowed, or blue.

I held the shower in my studio, since many of the guests were coworkers. This also allowed us to sneak in a dress fitting with the bride! But you could easily re-create this shower at any location. Because it was held at teatime, there was no big meal to prepare—so you don't even need a kitchen—and you can get all of the sewing supplies in a single trip to the craft store. All you need are needles, embroidery floss, a set of plain white linen napkins (I got ours from Ikea), and some scissors and pincushions. Wooden embroidery hoops are optional, but I thought they added a nice visual touch and helped with the sewing. I also bought pens with erasable ink, so guests could sketch out a monogram on the napkin first and stitch over it. (Another option is to write the initials lightly in pencil.)

I decided against making this party a sit-down meal because I didn't want the eating and drinking to take too much attention away from the main activity. I chose a few foods traditionally served at an afternoon tea and worked them into our color scheme: little lemon tarts, *macarons*, open-faced cucumber sandwiches for a springlike burst of green, and, of course, a signature cocktail: a blueberry mojito.

ven though I run a fashion design company, there are several women in the office who don't sew and are a little afraid of it. But as I explained to them, even if you have never sewn on a button, you can stitch a monogram—it's just writing with thread. And at its core, the point of a sewing circle isn't to impress the other guests with your stitching skills; it's to spend time with friends, which is another reason that I think it's a perfect activity for a shower. (If your guests don't know each other already, this is also a great way to help people instantly connect.) Because making things is a passion of mine, I also love how this theme becomes an opportunity to show how simple and enjoyable this can be. After the shower, even the most skeptical guests told me they didn't realize how easy—and fun—sewing could be.

This being a bridal shower, blue and white were natural choices for the color palette. When I was envisioning the look of the table, my mind went immediately to vintage Wedgwood china, which, in addition to being blue and white, has a nice old-fashioned quality that seemed perfect for this throwback-inspired gathering. I found all the china pieces at an antique store in upstate New York—they didn't match, but that was the point. I love the look of different patterns and textures when they are held together by a single color. Instead of flowers, I bought bunches of fresh herbs and stuck them in creamers and sugar bowls that I placed all around the table.

118

We held the shower in the early evening, so I chose food traditionally served at afternoon tea: sweets and finger sandwiches. Seeing as it was 5:00 p.m., I insisted everyone have a cocktail before we started sewing!

BLUEBERRY-KIWI MOJITO

Serves 8

INGREDIENTS
Lime Syrup
1 cup sugar
1 lime, thinly sliced

Cocktail
8 kiwifruits, peeled and sliced
1 cup fresh blueberries
40 fresh mint leaves
1 cup light (white) rum
½ cup fresh lime juice
Ice cubes
2 cups club soda
Fresh mint sprigs, for garnish

For the Lime Syrup: Combine the sugar, lime, and 1 cup water in a heavy medium saucepan. Bring to a boil over high heat, stirring often. Reduce the heat to medium-low and simmer, stirring occasionally, until reduced to 1 cup, about 15 minutes. Pour through a strainer into a bowl and let cool completely. (The syrup can be made up to 1 week ahead. Pour into a bottle or jar, then cover and refrigerate until ready to use.)

For the Cocktail: In a large pitcher, muddle half the kiwi slices, half the blueberries, and the mint leaves with the lime syrup. Stir in the rum and lime juice. (The cocktail base can be made up to 8 hours ahead; cover and chill until ready to use.)

Pour the mixture over ice in glasses. Top each drink with ¼ cup club soda. Garnish with mint sprigs and the remaining kiwi slices and blueberries, and serve.

LEMON CURD TARTLETS

If you're in a hurry, you can purchase baked mini tartlet shells from a gourmet foods store, fill them with lemon curd, and top with blueberries.

Makes 8

INGREDIENTS
Crust
1 ½ cups all-purpose flour
½ cup shelled pistachios, toasted
½ cup confectioners' sugar
¼ teaspoon salt
9 tablespoons unsalted butter, cut into small cubes and frozen
1 large egg, lightly beaten

Lemon Curd
3 or 4 lemons
1 ½ cups granulated sugar
½ cup (1 stick) unsalted butter, at room temperature
4 extra-large eggs
⅛ teaspoon salt
1 pint fresh blueberries

For the Crust: Combine the flour and nuts in a food processor and process until the nuts are finely ground. Add the sugar and salt and blend to incorporate. Add the butter and cut it in using on/off turns until the butter is in pea-size pieces. With the machine running, add the egg and pulse a few more times until the dough has just formed a ball. Turn the dough out onto a piece of plastic wrap; gather it into a ball and flatten it into disc. Wrap in the plastic wrap and refrigerate for 2 hours.

Divide the dough into eight balls. Press one dough ball into the bottom and evenly up the sides of each of eight 3-inch-diameter tartlet pans with removable bottoms. Use the tines of a fork to poke holes into the dough in several places. Freeze the tartlet shells for at least 30 minutes. (The tarlet shells can be made to this point up to 3 days ahead. Cover and keep frozen until ready to use.)

Preheat the oven to 350°F. Place the tartlet shells on a rimmed baking sheet. Bake for 20 minutes. Press down any bubbles in the crusts with the back of a spoon. Return to oven and bake until golden brown, about 5 minutes more. Let the tartlet shells cool, then remove them from the pans.

For the Lemon Curd: Finely grate the zest (yellow rind only) from the lemons. Juice the lemons and set aside ½ cup of the juice. Combine the lemon zest and sugar in a food processor. Using on/off turns, pulse until the zest is finely ground. Transfer the lemon sugar to a medium bowl and add the butter. Beat together with a hand mixer until light. Beat in the eggs, one at a time, then beat in the lemon juice and salt. Transfer the mixture to a heavy large saucepan. Cook over medium-low heat, stirring continuously, until it thickens, about 10 minutes (do not boil). Remove from the heat and let cool. Cover and refrigerate until cold, at least 4 hours. (The lemon curd can be prepared up to 2 days ahead. Keep refrigerated until ready to use.)

Fill a disposable plastic pastry bag with the lemon curd. Cut ½ inch off one bottom corner to create an opening. Pipe the lemon curd into the tartlet shells. (A piping bag is useful for filling tartlets, but you can also spread the filling into the shells using a small spoon.) Top the tartlets with blueberries.

The guests congregated in the showroom, where I had set up the food and "decorated" with dresses from the bridal line. After everyone had a bite to eat and something to drink, we retreated to a part of the room where I had set up chairs in a circle. To make things as easy as possible for the guests, I pre-threaded needles with three different shades of blue. I also demonstrated a few easy patterns on a stitch piece to give less experienced seamstresses guidance for creating a monogram for the bride. A stitch piece is a single piece of fabric on which you sew different stitches side by side to test out colors and patterns. It's something we use in our office when we are working on my collections.

The threads I chose were three different shades of blue, but in terms of the design of the monogram, the sky was the limit! It's best to pick threads in shades of a single color or in two contrasting colors, so the finished pieces go nicely together no matter what people end up stitching. But you can adapt the palette to the season, the bride's wedding colors, or her china—whatever you think suits her best. Other linens that make nice shower gifts are tea towels, hand towels, fabric coasters, cocktail napkins, pot holders, and aprons. Or you could get a few of each to create a full his-and-hers set with the couple's new initials.

ABOVE AND LEFT: For favors, I gave the guests mini sewing baskets with needles and thread, tomato pincushions, and thimbles. Hopefully these will encourage everyone to sew again!

OPPOSITE: Many of the girls in my office wear Lela Rose gowns to their weddings. Since this bride was having a small destination wedding, we did a last fitting during the shower so we could all see her in her gown.

Of course, I couldn't resist the opportunity to decorate my sidecar bike for this almost-married occasion. And Bobbin couldn't resist the temptation to jump in—literally—as best dog!

GINGHAM STYLE

A ROOFTOP CHICKEN FRY IN THE COUNTRY

As much as I love throwing parties in my New York apartment, there are some kinds of gatherings that an urban loft isn't well suited for, and a classic summer picnic is one of them. When the days start getting long and the afternoons become reliably warm and sunny, I begin dreaming about the leisurely weekend lunches I often hold at our house in upstate New York.

Not surprisingly, my entertaining style in the country is somewhat different from my style in the city. Rather than evening parties and seated dinners, the gatherings I hold upstate are often picnics and usually take place on Saturday or Sunday afternoons. Whereas in the city, I like to take control over the cooking and decorating, when we have houseguests upstate, I make lunch the activity of the day, and everyone staying with us pitches in with the cooking and preparations. The food and decor are more casual, and instead of progressing from cocktail hour to

appetizers to entrées to desserts, we serve the meal family-style and then spend the rest of the afternoon outdoors, relaxing and playing games until the sun goes down.

Since we do these lunches fairly frequently, I like to come up with a theme to make things feel more special and festive. Last summer, when I was starting to think about hosting a picnic, I was hit by the perfect lighthearted theme and dress code: "Gingham Style." I made a quick invitation using some picnic props, snapped a photo, and e-mailed it to the guests the week prior. This helped get everyone in the mood and reminded them to get their checks in order. Turning it into a chicken fry gave the menu focus and made it seem more exciting than a regular picnic. I often serve fried chicken when I'm upstate because it's the perfect picnic food, a reliable crowd-pleaser, and something that I wouldn't make in the city.

The guest list was simple: the family that would be staying with us over the weekend, plus a few friends and neighbors. I am always looking for unique touches that I can work into even the most casual meals, so I decided that instead of picnicking on the lawn, we'd have our meal on our house's green roof, which has an amazing view of the surrounding mountains and countryside.

We spent the morning of the picnic leisurely preparing the meal and walking around our property picking wildflowers and berries. When we were ready to eat, we lowered a bucket from the roof to hoist everything up to the picnic site. I bundled together colorful plates and gingham napkins with a paper band that I had written the menu on. Our checkered checks and bucolic surroundings provided just about everything we needed in terms of decor, so all I added were some buckets filled with the flowers we had picked that morning. The meal flowed into an afternoon of low-key outdoorsy activities, such as making daisy crowns, a spirited game of horseshoes, and swinging on our tree swing.

Making daisy crowns with my daughter is one of my favorite things to do on a lazy summer afternoon, and if you've never made one before (or haven't since you were a child), they're easier than they look. First, pick a bunch of daisies with nice long stems. Then use your fingernail to make a small slit in the middle of each stem. Take two daisies and slip the stem of one through the slit in the stem of the other, repeating until the crown is wide enough to go around your head. Then attach the two ends by slipping the stem of the last daisy into the slit in the stem of the first daisy.

WHISKEY SMASH

You can purchase simple syrup at a liquor store but I prefer to make it at home.

Serves 8

INGREDIENTS
56 fresh mint leaves
2 lemons, each cut into 8 wedges
8 tablespoons simple syrup

2 cups bourbon
Ice cubes
Crushed ice
8 fresh mint sprigs, for garnish

For the Simple Syrup: Bring 1 cup water and 1 cup sugar to a boil in a medium saucepan, stirring often. Boil for 1 minute, then remove from the heat and let cool completely. Cover and refrigerate up to 1 week.

For each Cocktail: In a shaker, muddle 7 mint leaves, 2 lemon wedges, and 1 tablespoon simple syrup. Add about 1 cup ice cubes, cover, and shake vigorously 4 or 5 times to release the juices and oils. Add ¼ cup bourbon to the shaker and shake again. Fill a tumbler glass halfway with crushed ice. Strain the cocktail mixture over the crushed ice. Garnish with a mint sprig and serve.

"Gingham style" perfectly captured the playful, casual mood I was trying to create. I worked gingham into everything I could think of, from the napkins and blanket we ate off of to the little checked ribbons I tied around the necks of the bottles to differentiate beer from root beer. Having a theme made the casual afternoon feel a little more special, and the sea of checks, plaids, and printed cotton looked picture-perfect against the green field behind us.

THIS PAGE: When I entertain at our country home, I give guests specific tasks that they can do at their leisure, such as squeezing limes for cocktails, chopping vegetables, and picking berries and wildflowers for the table. Making a meal together becomes a fun group activity and a way to spend time together with results that everyone can enjoy.

OPPOSITE: I did all of the shopping the day before so we could enjoy the morning at home. As always, local, seasonal produce featured heavily in the meal. Grilled corn with plenty of home-made herb butter is always on my summer picnic menu; I also serve the corn plain with chiles and cotija cheese on the side so people can doctor their cobs with as much spice as they like.

CRISPY FRIED CHICKEN

Serves 8

INGREDIENTS

⅔ cup plus 1 tablespoon
kosher salt

⅓ cup packed brown sugar

8 large garlic cloves, smashed

8 fresh thyme sprigs

2 tablespoons whole
black peppercorns

2 whole organic chickens,
each cut into 10 pieces

2 cups all-purpose flour

1 ½ teaspoons baking powder

1 ½ teaspoons cornstarch

1 teaspoon cayenne pepper

½ teaspoon freshly
ground black pepper

4 large eggs

4 cups buttermilk

Vegetable oil, for deep-frying

In a very large, deep pot, combine 2 quarts water with ⅔ cup of the
salt, the brown sugar, garlic, thyme sprigs, and peppercorns and stir to
dissolve the salt. Add the chicken pieces, submerging them in the brine.
Refrigerate at least 6 hours or overnight. Drain the chicken and pat dry.

Place a rack over a baking sheet. In a large bowl, combine the
flour, remaining 1 tablespoon salt, the baking powder, cornstarch,
cayenne, and black pepper. In another large bowl,
whisk together the eggs and buttermilk. Dredge one-
quarter of the chicken pieces in the buttermilk mixture,
then in the spiced flour. Shake off the excess flour.
Place the chicken pieces on the rack.

Preheat the oven to 300°F. Pour oil into a
heavy large pot to a depth of 4 inches. Heat the oil
over medium-high heat until it registers 325°F on a
deep-fry thermometer. When the oil is hot, fry 3 to 5
chicken pieces at a time (do not crowd the oil) until
golden brown and cooked through, turning them
occasionally, about 10 minutes, adjusting the heat as
necessary. (Reduce the heat if the chicken browns
too quickly.) Using tongs, transfer the chicken pieces
to a rimmed baking sheet and keep them warm
in the oven while you coat and fry the remaining
chicken pieces. Serve the chicken hot.

Fried chicken and biscuits is a classic Southern pairing. I like to add my own twist by rounding out the meal with a light, crunchy cabbage slaw— the brighter the better.

THIS PAGE: We could have carried everything to the roof ourselves, but what fun would that have been? Instead, my husband, Brandon, rigged a simple pulley system to get the picnic up to the roof, sending up the bucket when the chicken was crisp and piping hot. OPPOSITE: Printed menus aren't practical or expected at a picnic, but I think it's always nice to know what you are being served. My solution: write the afternoon's offerings across bands of craft paper and use them to make portable place settings. This makes it easier to be sure you've got the correct number of plates and utensils, and it's also fun for guests to pick up their little packages before the meal. I chose craft paper because it would be strong enough to hold the place settings together and easy to write on, but I made things festive by cutting the edges with pinking shears. The napkins were gingham, of course.

BUTTERMILK FRIED CHICKEN · CABBAGE + KOHLRABI SLAW
GRILLED CORN + FIXINS · BISCUITS + HONEY · MINT ICE CREAM ·
STRAWBERRY RHUBARB CRISP

BUTTERMILK
GRILLED CORN +

AN APPLE (OR PEAR,
OR STRAWBERRY, OR PEACH) A DAY

Fruit crumbles are my go-to dessert for summertime entertaining. They are crowd-pleasing, easy to throw together, require relatively basic ingredients (oats, sugar, butter), and are perfect for showcasing delicious local produce. (Bonus: They pair perfectly with ice cream.) Once you have a basic crumble recipe (like the one on page 152), you can adapt it for whatever fruit is currently in season: berries and rhubarb in the spring and early summer, stone fruit (peaches, plums, nectarines, cherries, apricots) in late summer, and apples or pear in the fall. When summer is at its peak and I have more fruit than my family and I can handle, I also like to make a variation of Rumtopf, a German dessert of fruit preserved in rum. I mix a pint of berries with a pound of peaches or nectarines and another pound of plums, and then layer in 2 ½ cups of sugar and a bottle of dark rum. The mixture needs to steep in a pantry (do not refrigerate) for a minimum of three weeks, but is best after twelve weeks—and will keep for up to a year. Serve it with ice cream, in cocktails, with cake at Christmastime, or use it in place of the Rum Roasted Stone Fruit in the trifle on page 179.

STRAWBERRY RHUBARB CRUMBLE

Serves 8

INGREDIENTS

2 quarts strawberries, hulled and quartered (about 4 cups)

4 to 6 stalks rhubarb, trimmed, cut into ½-inch pieces (about 3 cups)

1 cup sugar, divided in half

2 tablespoons fresh lemon juice

1 teaspoon vanilla extract

1 cup all purpose flour

1 teaspoon ground cinnamon

Large pinch of salt

½ cup (1 stick) chilled unsalted butter, cut into ½-inch pieces, plus more for greasing ramekins

½ cup chopped pecans

Vanilla ice cream

Preheat oven to 350°F. Butter eight 1- to 1 ½-cup ramekins. Combine strawberries and rhubarb in a large bowl. Add ½ cup of the sugar, lemon juice, and vanilla and toss to combine. Let stand until juicy, about 30 minutes.

Meanwhile, stir flour, remaining ½ cup sugar, cinnamon, and salt in a medium bowl to blend. Rub the butter into the flour mixture with fingertips or a pastry cutter until the mixture resembles coarse meal. Mix in the pecans.

Divide the strawberry mixture evenly among the prepared ramekins. Top it with the crumble mixture. Bake until the crumble is golden brown and the filling bubbles thickly, about 25 minutes. Serve warm with vanilla ice cream.

I have a set of eighteen napkins that I've embroidered with the names of weekend guests. Whenever friends or family come to visit us upstate, I add their names to one of the napkins. It's my version of a guestbook—the napkins are now filled with names, and they're a great conversation piece during meals.

152

HOSTING TIPS FOR HAPPY WEEKENDS

Even when meals are casual, a well-thought-out menu is always appreciated. I plan out all of the weekend's meals in advance and do the shopping on the way, so no one has to spend a lot of time driving back and forth to the store once we're out there.

Buying local not only supports the community, it's also a great way to show guests the character of your area. I get milk and fresh eggs from the neighboring farm and cheese from a local purveyor. I have even found a smokehouse nearby that sells smoked eels from the Delaware River, which we barbeque and eat on toast. People love to get to know a place through its unique local specialties.

I put pairs of slippers in each bedroom as a signal to guests that they can kick off their shoes and get comfortable immediately.

Rather than plan big outings, we like to spend our weekends with friends relaxing at home and playing games. When the weather is nice, we spend hours outdoors doing horseshoe tosses, making daisy crowns, and having egg races. For rainy days, a deck of cards always does the trick. We've even typed up instruction sheets for our favorite, a card game called "Oh Heck," for our guests to use.

Nothing is more welcoming than a platter or jar of homemade cookies. I get a batch going as soon as I arrive at the house, and I leave them on the table for people to snack on all weekend.

TEA-QUILA
A TEA PARTY WITH A TWIST

believe true style comes from creative, unexpected combinations and I love to play with contrasts. I'm a Southern blonde who lives in a quirky (to say the least) downtown loft and loves tequila. I'm a fashion designer known for dresses, floral prints, and bridal gowns who bikes to work every day in a dress and heels. My general goal, in work and in play, is to mix a refined uptown polish with idiosyncratic downtown fun. When it comes to entertaining, I find myself rejecting occasions in favor of inspiration and delighting in surprising guests with off-kilter touches. I love the pomp and circumstance of a formal gathering, but I've also never met a tradition that I didn't want to run my bike tires over. And no gathering oozes tradition quite like a ladies' tea.

The thought of spending a sober afternoon engaged in idle chitchat makes me yawn, which is exactly the reason why, when I decided to host a women-only gathering for some of my closest friends and customers, I

and be sure to
Wear your
Lela

couldn't resist taking the idea of a tea party and spicing it up—in this case, that turned out to be more like spiking it up. I held my "tea-quila" party in the rooftop garden of my friend Celerie's apartment, which has a view overlooking Central Park and was the perfect majestic uptown setting for me to inject some teatime mischief into. This event took place in early September so my guests would have one last opportunity to put on their colorful, springy Lela dresses before the cold set in. It was also right after I had shown my spring collection in New York, so I was in the mood for an afternoon of leisure—and cocktails.

Everything I did for this tea was about infusing unexpected fun into the clichés of formal entertaining. Celerie and I set the table with a mix of traditional pieces and some surprising tongue-in-cheek touches. We put antique teapots on platters and used them as vases, then added a bunch of silver flasks and colored glass liquor bottles. I rarely decorate with flowers—too expected for my taste—but here, hot pink cockscombs were the perfect way to express the ladylike and lively atmosphere. I painted plain white china in a plaid pattern taken from my spring collection and made napkins and ties for the servers out of a leftover floral fabric. Citrine is one of my favorite colors, as well as the color of our brand, and it was also an ideal backdrop for the bevy of multicolored flowery dresses. The cheekiest touches of all were the place cards I made for guests, each with their special "tipsy name" (Vodka Vivi, Saucy Shannon, Jug-a-Lug Jennifer), which was written in an ornate calligraphy script. When guests arrived looking their put-together best, we loosened up the ladies immediately with tea-inspired cocktails: "brewed" bourbon, iced "tea-quila," and a vodka-lemon concoction called a Tammy Collins. We served a playful menu of "toasted" finger sandwiches, "turn't" turnips and "trashed" radishes with vodka dipping sauce, and a messy, boozy trifle. The result was an afternoon of saucy, uninhibited fun during which no ladylike custom was left un-smashed.

I love to entertain at a friend's house because it gives me the chance to root around in their cabinets and closets for things to put together a table with. It is such fun to see what friends have bought and collected over the years, and put those things to use in a way that feels fresh and new—usually for both of us.

Grab a Cup
&
Spike it Up

I wanted the table to look elegant, sprinkled with accents of mischief. I bought a plain tea set on eBay and painted the pieces with ceramic paint. I also bought a bunch of antique silver flasks to decorate the table with—lest anyone forget what kind of tea this was—and made napkins using fabric leftover from my spring collection, which I had presented a few days earlier.

BREWED BOURBON
(ALSO KNOWN AS A NOR' EASTER)

Serves 8

INGREDIENTS
2 cups bourbon
½ cup (or more) fresh lime juice
½ cup maple syrup
Ice cubes
2 cups cold ginger beer
8 lime slices, for garnish

In a medium pitcher, stir together the bourbon, lime juice, and maple syrup to blend. Pour the mixture over ice in 8 rocks glasses and top each with ¼ cup ginger beer. Depending on the sweetness of the ginger beer, add a little more lime juice, if desired, to each drink. Garnish each drink with a lime slice and serve.

This party was girls-only—
except for Bobbin. This
get-together was a last
hurrah of summer, and
everyone pulled out the
stops with their outfits. I
always love seeing my
friends in Lela dresses,
but sometimes I forget to
check out what fabulous
shoes they pair them with!

Toasted Sandwich
deviled egg salad with old bay,
capers, red onion, watercress

EGG SALAD TOASTED TEA SANDWICHES

Serves 8

INGREDIENTS

8 hard-boiled eggs, peeled and cooled

¼ cup aioli or mayonnaise, plus more to spread

1 tablespoon Dijon mustard or stoneground mustard

4 slices crisp cooked bacon, crumbled

6 slices white sandwich bread

Fresh watercress sprigs

Halve the eggs, remove the yolks, and put them in a medium bowl. Coarsely chop the egg whites. Mix the aioli and mustard into the yolks and mash together well; mix in the chopped whites. Season with salt and pepper. (The egg salad can be made up to 1 day ahead. Cover and refrigerate until ready to use.)

When ready to serve, mix the bacon into the egg salad. Spread additional mayonnaise on each slice of bread. Top with some egg salad. Cut each slice into four squares. Garnish with watercress and serve.

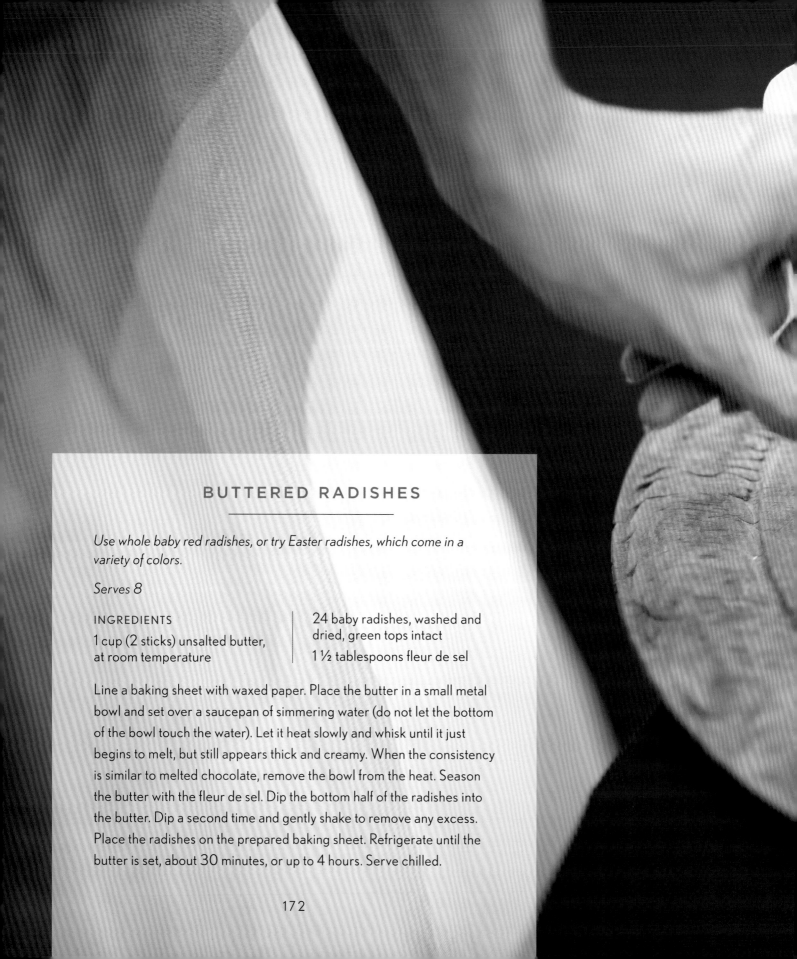

BUTTERED RADISHES

Use whole baby red radishes, or try Easter radishes, which come in a variety of colors.

Serves 8

INGREDIENTS

1 cup (2 sticks) unsalted butter, at room temperature

24 baby radishes, washed and dried, green tops intact

1 ½ tablespoons fleur de sel

Line a baking sheet with waxed paper. Place the butter in a small metal bowl and set over a saucepan of simmering water (do not let the bottom of the bowl touch the water). Let it heat slowly and whisk until it just begins to melt, but still appears thick and creamy. When the consistency is similar to melted chocolate, remove the bowl from the heat. Season the butter with the fleur de sel. Dip the bottom half of the radishes into the butter. Dip a second time and gently shake to remove any excess. Place the radishes on the prepared baking sheet. Refrigerate until the butter is set, about 30 minutes, or up to 4 hours. Serve chilled.

THIS PAGE: All of the dishes I served were twists on a traditional tea-party menu, riffs on cocktails and drinking, or both. We served "toasted" finger sandwiches (see page 171), turnips and radishes dipped in butter, salt, and vodka, shot glasses of ceviche, and several bracing cocktails we invented for the occasion.

RIGHT PAGE: No matter how dressy or casual the gathering I'm hosting, I always make place cards when there is a seated meal and use them as another opportunity to play up the event's theme. Here, I christened each guest with a "tea-quila name" for the afternoon, which I wrote in calligraphy on a petal pink card and placed in a gilded bamboo place-card holder.

Trifle is best served in a footed glass bowl, so guests can appreciate the drama of the colorful layers of fruit, cake, and cream. We served ours with *crème anglaise* on the side in a silver gravy boat so guests could "get sauced" on their own.

TRIFLE WITH BOOZY STONE FRUIT AND "GET SAUCED" CRÈME ANGLAISE

For an extra kick, substitute the rum-roasted fruit for fruit that's been steeped in alcohol for several months (see page 151).

Serves 8

INGREDIENTS

Sponge Cake

6 large eggs, at room temperature

1 cup (generous) sugar

½ teaspoon salt

1 cup cake flour

2 teaspoons grated lemon zest

Rum-Roasted Stone Fruit

1 pint mixed berries (such as raspberries, blackberries, and strawberries)

1 pound mixed peaches and nectarines, pitted, and cut into ½-inch- thick wedges

1 pound mixed plums, rinsed, pitted, and cut into ½-inch- thick wedges

2 ½ cups sugar

Juice from 1 lemon

½ cup dark rum

Trifle Cream

2 cups whole milk

½ vanilla bean, halved lengthwise, seeds scraped

3 large eggs
¾ cup sugar
6 tablespoons cornstarch
Pinch of salt
2 cups heavy cream, chilled
Unsprayed non-poisonous red flower petals
(such as rose or carnation; optional)

Crème Anglaise
2 cups whole milk
1 vanilla bean, halved lengthwise, seeds scraped
½ cup sugar
4 large egg yolks

For the Sponge Cake: Preheat the oven to 350°F. Butter an 11 x 17 x 1-inch jelly roll pan. Line the bottom with parchment paper; butter and flour the paper.

In a large bowl using a hand mixer, beat the eggs, sugar, and salt until very light and fluffy, about 12 minutes. Gently fold in the flour and lemon zest. Spread the batter over the prepared pan. Bake until the cake springs back when lightly pressed in the center, about 15 minutes. Run a small sharp knife around the edges of the cake to release it from the pan. Turn the cake out onto a sheet of aluminum foil; let the cake cool completely. (The cake can be prepared up to 1 day ahead. Cover and set aside at room temperature until ready to use.)

For the Rum-Roasted Stone Fruit: Preheat oven to 350°F. Place fruit on a baking sheet and sprinkle with sugar and lemon juice. Roast fruit in oven until soft and juicy, about 25 minutes. Transfer the fruit to a bowl and mix in rum. Refrigerate up to 2 days.

For the Trifle Cream: Combine the milk and vanilla bean pod and seeds in a heavy large saucepan. Bring to simmer. Remove from the heat, cover, and let steep for 1 to 2 hours.

Return the milk mixture to simmer. Whisk the eggs, sugar, cornstarch, and salt in a medium bowl

until smooth. Gradually whisk in the hot milk mixture. Return the mixture to the same saucepan. Cook over medium heat, whisking continuously, until the mixture boils and becomes very thick, about 3 minutes. Continue cooking for 1 minute longer, whisking continuously. Transfer the trifle cream to a bowl and remove the vanilla pod. Place plastic wrap directly against the surface of the cream to prevent a skin from forming. Refrigerate until very cold, at least 2 hours. Just before assembling the trifle, in a large bowl using a hand mixer, beat the heavy cream to soft peaks. Fold the whipped cream into the trifle cream. Cover and refrigerate until ready to use, or up to 4 hours.

For the Crème Anglaise: Place a strainer over a medium bowl and set it over a larger bowl filled with ice. Combine the milk and vanilla bean pod and seeds a heavy large saucepan. Bring the mixture just to a simmer over medium-low heat. Whisk the sugar and egg yolks in a large bowl just until combined. Gradually whisk in half the hot milk mixture. Pour the mixture back into the saucepan and cook over medium heat, stirring continuously with a wooden spoon, until the sauce has thickened slightly, 4 to 5 minutes. Pour the sauce through the strainer. Let cool, stirring occasionally. Cover and refrigerate the sauce until ready to use, up to 3 days ahead.

To Assemble: Peel the parchment off the cake. Roughly tear the cake into 2-inch pieces. Spoon some of the trifle cream into the bottom of a large decorative glass bowl or trifle dish. Top with some of the torn pieces of cake, followed by a layer of the boozy fruit. Repeat several times to fill the bowl. The top layer should be the cream with some of the fruit drizzled on top. Sprinkle with flower petals, if desired. To serve, scoop trifle into serving bowls. Using a large spoon or ladle, top with crème anglaise.

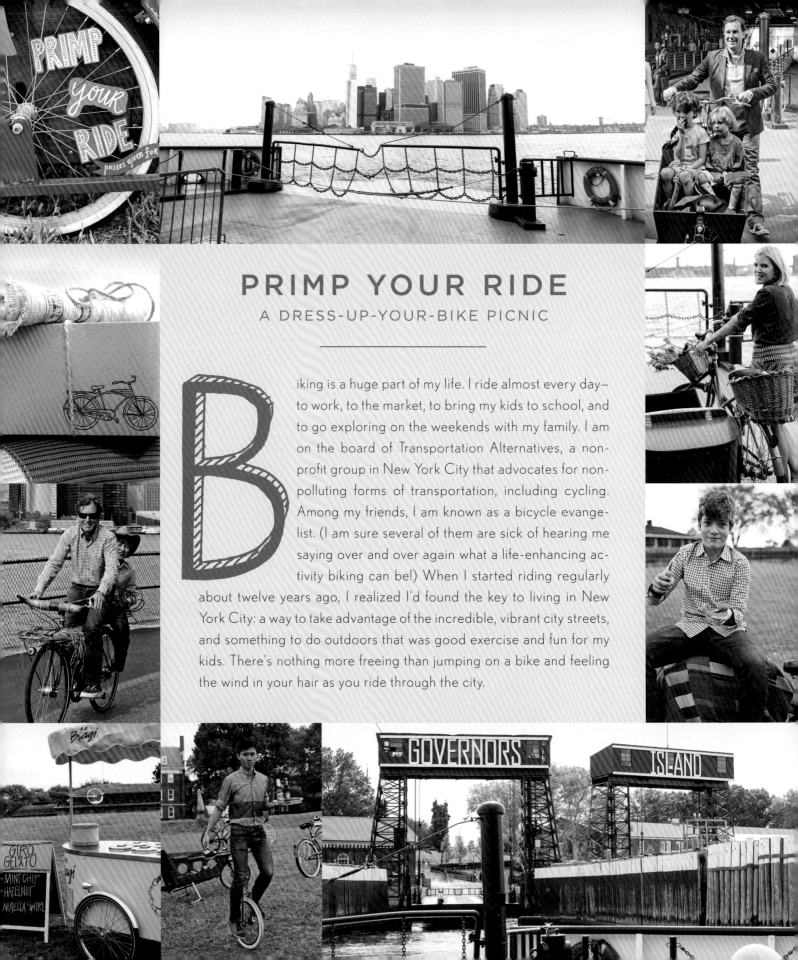

PRIMP YOUR RIDE
A DRESS-UP-YOUR-BIKE PICNIC

Biking is a huge part of my life. I ride almost every day—to work, to the market, to bring my kids to school, and to go exploring on the weekends with my family. I am on the board of Transportation Alternatives, a non-profit group in New York City that advocates for non-polluting forms of transportation, including cycling. Among my friends, I am known as a bicycle evangelist. (I am sure several of them are sick of hearing me saying over and over again what a life-enhancing activity biking can be!) When I started riding regularly about twelve years ago, I realized I'd found the key to living in New York City: a way to take advantage of the incredible, vibrant city streets, and something to do outdoors that was good exercise and fun for my kids. There's nothing more freeing than jumping on a bike and feeling the wind in your hair as you ride through the city.

Yet while I see every reason and then some to start biking, I don't see riding a bike as a reason to compromise your style. I ride all over the city with only the occasional concession of a pair of flats. In fact, instead of interfering with my style, my bikes have become an extension of it, and I've given each of my three bicycles specialized touches—building one out with a sleigh to carry home my farmers market hauls (it's also perfect for Christmastime decor), and kitting another out with a sidecar that my kids love to ride in so that I can regularly (and fashionably) take them wherever I want to go.

One of my other great New York City loves is Governors Island, a car-free national park a short ferry ride from Lower Manhattan. It is one of the most unique and serene places in the entire city, and one of my favorite places to go with my family for a bike ride. I decided to combine these two passions and invite my friends and their bikes to Governors Island for an early autumn picnic. The invitation called for guests to "primp their rides," which was my not-so-subtle suggestion that my friends—and their bikes—dress their best. Color, creativity, and props were all welcome; spandex was not.

Perhaps more than any other party in this book, this one epitomizes my overall philosophy of entertaining that the best parties come from inspiration, not occasions. This is also probably the most casual party I've thrown, and one that's easy to replicate. All you need is a public park, simple picnic food that you can make or buy, and a group of friends who are game for adventure.

DO'S AND DON'TS FOR RIDING IN STYLE

DO wear a skirt, the fuller the better. You won't have to worry about wrinkling a pant leg or getting it dirty on a bike chain, and skirts look great on a bike. But leave the minis at home.

DON'T worry about your hair. The windblown look is always in.

DO stock up on wedges. They're the perfect cycling shoe—even better than flats—because the height makes it easier to pedal.

DON'T even think about spandex. Wear your real clothes.

DON'T forget your basket. Having something to keep your belongings in not only looks better than stuffing everything in your pockets–it's safer too. Find a basket that goes with your bike's look, or decorate one yourself.

DO come prepared. I keep a spare pair of gloves in every bag I own, in case the weather turns cool or rainy. I also keep a bungee cord or two to use when the basket fills up, as it often does!

One of the best parts of the party was seeing what people came up with to decorate their bikes with. Challenging my guests to primp their rides ensured that we were surrounded by plenty of style, color, and fun.

THIS PAGE: Guests provided almost all the decoration we needed with their spiffed-up bicycles. From a colorful fabric-covered bike with a basket of autumn flowers to themed rides like the Champagne Cycle and Wheels of Cheese—a bike equipped with all the fixings for a cheese plate, including baguettes strapped to the posts—there was enough color and creativity in the primping to carry the day. OPPOSITE: I took a cue from professional cycling by creating a podium to celebrate the most creative primpers and awarded each with a new bike bell.

Lunch boxes simplified the food prep and cleanup, a must when you are throwing a party in a public space. I assembled the boxes at the picnic site before guests arrived and stamped each one with a bike stamp I found at a stationery store. Instead of printing menus, I handwrote the list of picnic fare inside each box with black marker.

- SMOKED DUCK BREAST & SOUR
CHERRY BAGUETTE
- PROSCIUTTO BAGUETTE w/ BLUE CHEESE & FIGS
- DILL PICKLE
- NORTH FORK POTATO CHIPS
- SEA SALTED BROWNIE

My table decor was minimal and efficient, with a few simple touches—wild-flowers placed in wicker bike baskets, and a craft-paper "tablecloth" that was made by covering my bike tires with black paint and riding over it—that kept us stylish and on-theme.

197

I combed the city for bicycle-related food vendors who came over on the ferry with us to set up by our picnic spot. I even recruited a unicyclist I saw performing in Washington Square Park to serve drinks!

BEER

LEMONADE

BIVALVES BY BICYCLE

THE FIFTH WHEEL

Serves 8

INGREDIENTS
10 cups cubed seedless watermelon
2 large cucumbers,
peeled and cut into chunks
1 ⅓ cups vodka
½ cup fresh lime juice
¼ cup honey, plus more as needed
Ice cubes
Cucumber slices, for garnish

Set a large, fine-mesh sieve over a large bowl. Combine the watermelon cubes and cucumber chunks in a separate large bowl. Working in batches, puree the watermelon and cucumber in a blender. Pour the puree through the sieve, pressing on the solids with a rubber spatula; discard the solids in the sieve. Transfer the puree to a large pitcher or drinks dispenser and add the vodka, lime juice, and honey, stirring to dissolve the honey. Adjust the sweetness by adding more honey, if desired. Fill tumbler glasses with ice. Pour the drink over ice and garnish with cucumber slices.

GIRO
DI
GELATO

- MINT CHIP
- HAZELNUT
- NUTELLA SWIRL

When I'm planning a party, I like to brainstorm ideas that go with my theme, and I love coming up with special names and funny word alliterations that I can work into the food and drink. I rented this bike-powered gelato cart for the day, which I christened the Giro di Gelato, a reference to the famous Italian bike race.

RECIPE INDEX

ACKNOWLEDGMENTS

Writing a book about entertaining and throwing a party have at least one thing in common: they both rely on the presence and participation of others, so getting the right mix is key. I would not have been able to pull it all off without the help and tireless support from the following:

Jill Cohen, who guided me through the book-making process from soup to nuts, and made an excellent party guest on more than a few occasions.

Caitlin Leffel, my writer, Kathleen Jayes, my editor, and Rizzoli's publisher, Charles Miers, who turned an idea into a book. Another thanks to Jeanne Kelly, for her help on the recipes.

Doug Turshen, our designer, and Steve Turner, for wading through dozens and dozens of photographs to come up with a layout that fit me perfectly.

Quentin Bacon, Melanie Acevedo, and Heather Weston: thank you for your incredible eye in capturing these events. It could not have been easy—you are all amazingly talented!

Sam, my right hand man, for his endless stream of creative ideas, energy, and willingness to "get it done" no matter how ridiculous the task (i.e., riding a cargo bike literally piled high with stuff and navigating the NYC streets).

My wonderful staff—past and present—at Lela Rose: Akira, Amy, Arianna, Betsy, Caitlin, Caroline, Chanel, Courtney, Demi, Ellen, Erin, Felicia, Hiral, Jackie, Jenny, Kait, Karen, Leonora, Linda, Marianna, Mimi, Pablo, Susie, Tricia, and many of our interns.

To my parents, Deedie and Rusty Rose, who have been a constant inspiration in too many ways to recount here and who raised me with love and in a home where fun ruled the day. An extra special thanks to my mother, whose tireless creativity and quest to build things had me constantly crafting as a child.

Thanks to my sister-in-law Catherine Rose, for always being there to bounce ideas around with me as well as her witty way with words.

To Andrew, our live-in friend, for due to proximity, there wasn't a task he could get away from, ever!

To my friends who appear in these pages, thank you for all the years of gamely going along with my ever-more-unusual party themes—and for always dressing the part, no matter how outlandish.

Grey and Rosey: together you are one of the main reasons that every day is an occasion, full of endless fun and laughs (with a few tears added in).

And finally, to Brandon: I couldn't have done this without you. You were always willing to drop everything to help me get this book done. I love you and I thank you!!!

First published in the United States of America in 2015
by Rizzoli International Publications, Inc.
300 Park Avenue South
New York, NY 10010
www.rizzoliusa.com

All photography by Quentin Bacon except:
Heather Weston: pages 9, 12-13, 16-26, 27 right, 28-29, 182-200, 201 right, 202-203
Melanie Acevedo: pages 2-3, 30-55,56-75
Elizabeth D. Herman: page 4
Hal Horowitz: page 5
Daniel Krieger: endpapers and reverse of front endpapers

Text by Caitlin Leffel

2015 2016 2017 2018 / 10 9 8 7 6 5 4 3 2 1

Distributed in the U.S. trade by Random House, New York

Printed in China

Design by Doug Turshen and Steve Turner

ISBN-13: 978-0-8478-4629-0

Library of Congress Control Number: 2015936969